GRAPHIC DESIGNER'S COLOR HANDBOOK

ROCKPORT

GRAPHIC DESIGNER'S COLOR HANDBOOK

Choosing and Using Color from Concept to Final Output

GLOUCESTER MASSACHUSETTS

ROCKPORT PUBLISHERS

RICK SUTHERLAND AND BARB KARG

DESIGNED BY PETER KING & COMPANY

First published in the United States of America by Rockport Publishers, Inc.
33 Commercial Street
Gloucester, Massachusetts 01930-5089
Telephone: (978) 282-9590
Fax: (978) 283-2742
www.rockpub.com

Library of Congress Cataloging-in-Publication Data
Karg, Barbara.
  Graphic designer's color handbook : choosing and using color from concept to final output / Barb Karg and Rick Sutherland.
     p. cm.
  ISBN 1-56496-935-5
  1. Color in design—Handbooks, manuals, etc.
  2. Color printing—Handbooks, manuals, etc.
  I. Sutherland, Rick. II. Title.
  NK1548 .K375 2003
  701'.85—dc21   2002011283

Some images © 2000—www.arttoday.com

Design: Peter King & Company
Cover: Blackcoffee Design Inc.

Printed in China

This book is dedicated to our wonderful families and friends, who color our world on a daily basis. And to all designers and printers, who take the gray matter in our heads and turn it into a kaleidoscope of brilliant color.

CONTENTS

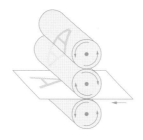

CHAPTER 06

COLOR ON THE WEB

CHAPTER 05 CONTINUED

INTRODUCTION

ONE OF THE MANY FASCINATING DISCOV-ERIES WE MADE while researching and writing the *Graphic Designer's Color Handbook* is that graphic design and communications media have for centuries been a far more intrinsic influence on the evolution of our society than we ever imagined.

Johannes Gutenburg's creation of movable type in the fifteenth century made information and knowledge accessible to the masses, but this is an over-simplification of a revolutionary process that profoundly appealed to human responses and visual interests. While Gutenburg's invention created a means for mass-producing the printed word, it also created an enduring medium for producing emotionally evocative and effective color design, as evidenced by the brilliant illustrations of Gutenburg's early Bibles still in existence.

We are blessed with an amazing visual sensibility that serves not simply as a biological necessity for survival but also as a means of highlighting, analyzing, and appreciating the modern world. It is this very sensibility that the graphic designer speaks to by creating imagery that appeals to our colorful and inquisitive nature. Without the influence of graphic designers, the aesthetic and intellectual growth of society would be clouded by shades of gray.

away, but it does offer the opportunity to distance yourself from the pack. Excellent design and execution of color has been done and will always be done, by those who understand and take full advantage of the remarkable processes available today.

The purpose of this book is to offer meaningful insights into the world of color graphic reproduction in real-world settings. Our goal is to provide practical, hardworking information that will serve you professionally by helping you better serve your clientele. It's a colorful world, and that world can be conquered by learning about the color process and, above all, using your imagination and creativity to bring colorful designs to fruition.

The accessibility of computers, graphics programs, and the Internet is creating a combination of challenges and opportunities for graphic designers. Increased accessibility has diluted some elements of the design market, and many people with a modicum of talent and experience have invested thousands of dollars on computers and programs, and announced themselves to be "graphic designers." Our opinion of this concept is the same as we would imagine Gutenburg's reaction might have been upon finding that his Bibles were being industriously illustrated by a stablehand who had recently purchased a cheap box of paints. This is a technological trend that will not go

THE PRINCIPLES OF COLOR

UNDERSTANDING COLOR IS THE KEY TO SUCCESSFUL GRAPHIC DESIGN, whether it's in or out of the digital world. Color is empowering, but it's also unpredictable because it's subject to so many variables from print to print, monitor to monitor, press to press, and domestic to international locales. Designers must learn how to balance the variables, mixing and matching colors so that a project is eye-catching and satisfying to a client.

All successful graphic designers become students of color. Every color has unique properties and problems. The trick is learning how to mix and match.

Color is subjective. Ten people could stare at this plate of chocolate chip cookies and describe the colors several different ways: brown, tan, ocher, beige, sepia, chestnut, mahogany—which do you see?

Color Theory:
WHAT DO YOU SEE?

AT A MONDAY MORNING MEETING, the production manager of a design agency holds up a picture containing a red square. Seated around the table are ten graphic designers. He asks the designers to write down the square's color, then reads each answer aloud: "Cherry, burgundy, Bombay, pimento, burnt orange, magenta, tomato, mauve, rose, and Pantone 186."

People agree on color as often as they agree on whose grandmother makes the best chocolate chip cookies. The above scenario is a typical color conundrum, whether between designer and client, sales rep and prepress operator, or broker and printer. Color brings life to the world around us, but it is subjective, and if there is one guiding rule, it's that one person's crimson is another's cranberry.

When you think of color, what first comes to mind? Your favorite color? The color of your car or your dog? Maybe it's the color of the jacket you're wearing.

The principles and theories regarding color are well researched, in fields as diverse as art, sales, and psychology. Colors can be loud, calm, fresh, neutral, dark, rich, stimulating, or mysterious. They can be vibrant or muted, warm or cool, and they are used in every imaginable combination. This diversity is particularly evident in the art world, where personal and professional opinions about color are rampant.

From ancient times to the modern age, color has played an important role in the visual arts. When gazing on the art and architecture of past civilizations, you can't help but become entranced by the lush, verdant colors artisans used to solidify their place in history. Artists from Egypt, Greece, Rome, and China created colorful images that remain beautiful and expressive thousands of years later. The true brilliance of their creations is that they understood how color works on the mind and in the environment. They learned how to combine colors, and how to apply them in abundance or in more subtle ways.

Color means different things to different people around the world. In some societies, colors are dictated by tradition and customs, such as wearing a white or red wedding dress. Certain colors are considered sacred, while others are forbidden. Everyone has a theory about color—its uses and abuses. Ultimately, how you think about color is personal. You will increase your value as a graphic designer by honing the color theories and instincts that you develop. Learn from past and present masters by studying their successes and failures, and in time, you'll become your own best color critic.

Artists and artisans understood the effectiveness of melding colors to create conceptual designs long before the advent of modern color theories and technical explanations of light waves and color spectrums.

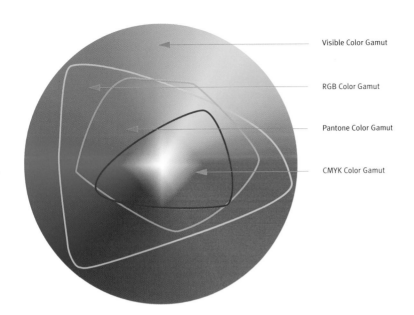

Visible Color Gamut

RGB Color Gamut

Pantone Color Gamut

CMYK Color Gamut

The color gamut of computer monitors is a fraction of the color range that the human eye can perceive. The color gamut for CMYK printing is even less, with a range of about four thousand colors, compared with the nearly ten million we can see in nature.

Running
the Gamut

COLOR GAMUT IS A TERM that describes the range of colors that can be produced by any given process or device, such as computer monitors or proofing systems. The dynamic range of human vision is about ten million colors, far greater than any known printing process can reproduce. This number is elastic and depends on the visual acuity of the individual. Interestingly enough, visual color deficiency—or color blindness—is far more prevalent among men, with 7 percent of the male population having some element of the condition. About 0.4 of 1 percent of women are similarly affected. This can be useful to bear in mind when you're reviewing proofs in a group or asking a press operator to make minor color adjustments on press.

Inabilities for some people to recognize minor changes in reds, blues, and yellows are not uncommon, and subtle color alterations in any or all of these colors that may be very apparent to one person, may appear to be unchanged to another. Having your color vision tested can be interesting and enlightening. The Internet contains a number of sites that offer simplified color testing programs. In depth color vision tests are also available from opticians.

Understanding that these often minute variations in individual color acuity are a fact of life can help relieve the sometimes frustrating process of trying to convince a client or press operator that the variations you see really exist, even if they don't see it exactly the same way you do.

Visual Adaptation

Our sense of sight is incredibly adaptive and works in conjunction with our brains to provide us with rational visual information. The adaptation illustration shown here is one example of how our vision helps us to keep our world in perspective.

This chromatic adaptation illustration demonstrates the fluidity of human vision and our eyes' ability to compensate for our environment. The left half of the fruit image appears too yellow, while the right half is too blue.

Now, stare at the black dot in the center of the yellow/blue adapting patches for thirty seconds without wavering. Then look at the black spot in the center of the fruit image. You'll notice that the two halves nearly match.

When you play with color, you walk a fine line between method and madness. So how do you know which colors are best? This plate shows how colors can work well together. The cool blues and blacks complement the warm oranges and reds. Yellow ties it all together.

Colors can be ritualistic, spiritual, and superstitious, but, above all, colors trigger emotion. The soft hues and surrealistic color transitions in this photograph have a calming, dreamlike effect.

Choosing and Using Color

WHETHER YOU'RE NEW to the design field or an experienced professional, color can be a tough customer. On any color job, you must strike a balance among a wide range of variables, such as hue, density, and saturation. How you choose and use color has much to do with instinct and experimentation.

Playing with color is much like choosing sides in *Star Wars*. When you're one with the Force, everything looks bright and hopeful, but when you dip into the dark side, it all becomes murky and chaotic. To become a successful color connoisseur, you need to understand the psychology and evolution of color. Practice combining colors; learn about hue, saturation, and density; and above all, fine-tune your color instincts.

Color Psychology

WHAT MAKES PEOPLE CHOOSE the colors that surround them? Is it a random choice, a conscious choice, or a subconscious choice? Perhaps, it's a combination of all three. We choose colors for many reasons, but most commonly because they are pleasing to the eye, they blend well with our surroundings, and even because they bring out the color of our eyes. But again, it's all about perception. Just because we like a certain color, doesn't mean anyone else will. Beauty, in this case, is definitely in the eye of the beholder

Color Perception

THE PERCEPTION OF COLOR is further complicated by the fact that colors mean different things to different people around the world. Colors are often associated with a variety of events or occurrences, including rites of passage, Mother Nature, loyalty, illness, spiritual enlightenment, and superstition. In Western culture, for example, white symbolizes cleanliness, virtue, and chastity, whereas in China, white is associated with mourning and grief.

Some colors, such as black, have negative connotations that are hard to dispel: "The dark side," "blacklisted," "the Black Plague," "black magic." Conversely, green evokes positive notions such as energy, life, growth, and money. "The grass is always greener…" is a state of mind often associated with green.

The psychology of color is subject to extreme differences of opinion. To prove this, ask several of your colleagues to write down objects or phrases associated with a certain color. When you read the answers, an interesting dynamic will emerge. For example, list everything you associate with red, and you'll run the gamut from roses, to stop signs, blood to tomatoes, red alerts and "seeing red." It's a color that suggests heat, love, passion, and danger. In symbolic terms, red is a warm color that in many cultures symbolizes strength and power. Whether consciously or not, individuals have innate and specific reactions to color.

Red is a highly visible color that traditionally symbolizes strength, passion, and power. With its thousands of shades and hues, red is also a color that people seldom agree on. The differences in tone can be subtle or dramatic, as these three images illustrate.

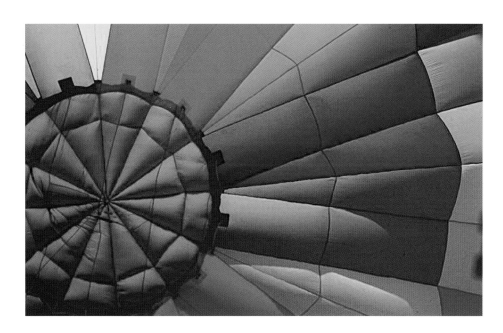

Large percentages of the four process colors can lead to dramatic, highly saturated images. In this image, 80 to 90 percent magenta is mixed with the same amount of yellow to create a deep, vibrant red.

The meaning and symbolism of colors vary by culture, but the following values often associated with specific colors:

RED:
passion, strength, power, danger

YELLOW:
playfulness, wisdom, optimism, jealousy

ORANGE:
creativity, warmth, adventurousness

GREEN:
healing, life, prosperity, regeneration, nurturing

BLUE:
loyalty, integrity, rejuvenation, trustworthiness, sadness

PURPLE:
royalty, mysticism, imagination

BROWN:
earth, nature, stability, balance

WHITE:
chastity, purity, virtue

BLACK:
mystery, death, rebirth, determination

In psychological terms, the values associated with certain colors can have a huge impact on the look and feel of a project. Some colors can project beauty, such as the reds, yellows, oranges, and browns of autumn. The deep hues of purple and blue can project richness, royalty, and elegance.

The meaning and use of colors will have a guaranteed impact on your projects—one way or another. Working with color will turn you into an amateur color psychologist, and the more experience and insight you glean out of a client's reactions, the better prepared you'll be for the next color challenge.

Some ancient societies believed in the healing capacity of color; while red was thought to stimulate energy, blue helped to cure colds and reduce bouts of hay fever. Even though this concept is regarded with a certain amount of skepticism in modern sociey, premature babies with jaundice are often treated and cured by exposure to blue light, which can trigger positive metabolic reactions.

One interesting attempt at using color to influence behavior is the bubble gum pink color sometimes used in jail and prison holding cells. The color seems to quell violent behavior, although studies have indicated that the effect is relatively short term.

An infinite number of intangible color associations will trigger a variety of responses in individuals. Traumatic events associated with a particular color can permanently affect an individual's reaction to that color. A sense of well being is often experienced by people who subconciously associate related colors, much the same way that the smell of baking cookies is reminiscent of soothing childhood memories.

When it comes to color, digital technology has opened a Pandora's box. Not long ago, designers manipulated color images without a color monitor. This frog, with its many percentages of greens, would have been nearly impossible to color correct on a grayscale display.

Color Evolution

BACK IN THE STONE AGE of graphic design and production, before computer systems became commonplace, color artwork went to press in numerous ways. Colors were specified on tissue overlays, cut out of rubyliths, or even drawn in colored pencil accompanied by pages of scribbled directions.

From the time the job left your hands, until the first proofs arrived from the printer, you held your breath. Often, yellow became butterscotch, your reds turned to pink, and that lush fern green transmuted into something commonly associated with nausea.

These days, you still hold your breath when delivering a job to the printer, and you still lose sleep wondering if the pale coral band bleeding off the top of each page should have been red. However, the processes you use to create, select, and display your colors from prepress to finished product have changed dramatically.

Designers now learning the trade have benefited from growing up with sophisticated hardware and software. However, if you've been around long enough to remember rubyliths, you probably found the digital color transition frustrating and time consuming, as all of the tried-and-true color palettes you developed over the years now required different percentages and specifications. Matters weren't helped by the primitive state of early desktop hardware. Because color monitors were small and expensive, many pioneering designers got by with monochrome displays, specifying color percentages on screens that could show only shades of gray. The trick was to create a digital file containing swatches with known color percentages, and then have it printed in color. You could then use the printed colors as visual references.

Anything related to color takes practice. Even Michelangelo had plenty of screw-ups on the Sistine Chapel before pronouncing it a masterpiece. Draw from your background, create samples, and build new color bases. You already know that greatness is the result of experimentation.

While color has evolved on many different levels, one factor remains constant. Color is an expensive commodity, and when used improperly, it is costly to repair. As you'll see in following chapters, you can employ many solutions to ensure proper color selection and display. But you need to understand how color works, both mentally and digitally. Rubyliths and tissue overlays served us well, but they pale in comparison to a whiz-bang color palette, a Pantone deck, and a 21-inch color monitor.

Understanding color balance will help you avoid making bad color choices. The right side of the ferns may look reasonable on the screen, but in reality, half of the yellow was eliminated due to some heavy-handed color manipulation.

Mastering color takes time and practice, but the best designers learn to experiment with different levels of CMYK to create new combinations and appearances. Sometimes, the most striking images are created by accident. Side-by-side comparisons of the flower and entryway show how different an image can become when all of the yellow is removed.

Color Confidence

THE BEST DESIGNERS exude a well-developed confidence when it comes to color. They've studied how colors work on the page and in digital form. They've learned to mix their own colors and create color palettes. Most importantly, they've learned about the printing process. It cannot be overstated: A designer who wants to be successful with color must learn how the printing process works.

Many designers don't have a clue about what happens to their project once it arrives in the printer's hands. All they know is that the FedEx driver collects the package and delivers it to printing land, where Merlin magically colors and prints everything to perfection. It's a sad and fatal tale. Don't hesitate to ask questions of your printing representatives. You will gain valuable insight into the process, along with immeasurable confidence when communicating with clients.

Chapter 4 examines this process in-depth. Learning the mechanics of color is important, but it is equally important to learn how printers will handle your project. Color experience is a valuable commodity among everyone in design, print, and Web production. If you don't have the confidence to produce color, other designers will, and as a result, their clients and printers will be more confident in the final product.

Find Out What the Client *Really* Wants

Successful color work requires careful communication between designer and client or employer. Miscommunication can burn budgets and scar reputations. Before beginning any color project, be certain that everyone is envisioning the same color. You can do this using a Pantone book, CMYK color swatches, or other color references.

THERE IS NOTHING MORE EDUCA-TIONAL—or amusing—than watching the color dance between client and designer as they discuss a job. It's a tense and uncomfortable time for both parties, as neither can agree on a hue, shade, tint, or density.

Every designer on the planet has endured the following situation. After weeks of preliminary meetings, the designer presents several logos to the client, who chooses the one they like. However, they request that the letters be royal blue. The next week, the designer gleefully presents the new logo, but the client winces in horror: "I said 'royal blue' for the lettering. That's not royal blue." The designer takes a long look at the lettering and determines that it's definitely a deep royal blue.

Sheepishly, the designer retrieves a color swatch book and points out the royal blue. The client skims through the book, selects a sky blue, plunks it down in front of the designer, and adamantly states, "*That* is royal blue."

The best advice any graphic designer can heed is to find out exactly what your client wants. In addition to calming your color fears, it will save time and production costs, while demonstrating your professionalism.

As a rule, always have color samples, swatches, or a Pantone deck on hand to present to your client. Ascertain what kind of look they're striving to achieve. If it's an advertisement in a retirement magazine, garish colors are most likely inappropriate. For an annual report, they may want to use corporate colors. The best approach is to listen and give them space and time to select the colors they're looking for. If they ask for recommendations, give them several choices. If a client changes their mind faster than their socks, run a color proof page with a variety of colors and let them choose the one they like. It's important to remember that battling with your client by voicing radical color opinions, or by being stubborn about their color choices, will most likely cost you an account.

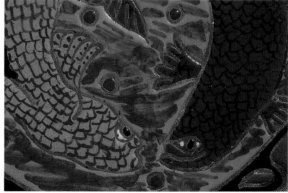

The Effects of Ambient Lighting

LIGHTING HAS A SIGNIFICANT effect on the way you and your clients see color. Many designers create a work environment that provides a great deal of natural light, which can be ideal for accurately creating, choosing, and viewing colors. Clients and readers often don't have the luxury or need to work in natural light, and much printed material is viewed under the harsh fluorescent lighting common to modern offices.

Fluorescent lighting is generally colder and bluer than natural light, and thus tends to emphasize cool colors and subdue warm ones. Incandescent lighting tends to be more yellow and, thus, enhances warmer colors. Natural light, which is replicated in viewing booths and on pressroom viewing tables, is primarily neutral and creates minimal color cast. A pale yellow image that matches a color swatch under controlled lighting can virtually disappear under fluorescent lights, an effect known as *metamerism*.

Ambient lighting can have a significant impact on how your color images appear. Reflective images, such as this example, appear to have different colors under various lighting conditions.

These images illustrate the
effect of metamerism.

The four red squares are all the
same color, but when seen
under incandescent light and
natural light, the differences
are unmistakable.

Metamerism

METAMERISM, as noted previously, occurs when objects match under certain lighting conditions but don't match under others. Proofs and press sheets produced with different pigments, dyes, and substrates can appear to be good matches in controlled natural light, but will be dissimilar under fluorescent or incandescent lighting. When proofing and press checking critical color matches, it's best to view the materials under different light sources. Stepping back a few feet from a viewing booth—and into the fluorescent lighting of most pressrooms—can provide a good representation of how a press sheet will appear in the office.

In this example, the identical blue square is shown under different lighting conditions. The square on the left is shown under incandescent, the middle square under fluorescent light, and the one on the right under natural light.

It's never too soon for a designer to discuss these issues with a client so that they have a reasonable understanding of the many ways that light sources visually affect color images. Sharing this knowledge will go a long way in assuring your clients that you have their best interests in mind and that voodoo doesn't play a part in the process. This is also a fact of life that good print reps and press operators should be intimately familiar with.

Using Common Sense

GRAPHIC DESIGNERS, like most creative folks, can be an assertive bunch, and everyone has an opinion. Some go down in flames as a result of stubborn pride. But the most successful designers can attribute their success to being open minded, learning from their mistakes, and using common sense.

Working with color is a privilege, not a curse. If you approach it with that attitude, you've won half the battle. While color can definitely push the limits of your patience, nothing is more gratifying than feasting your eyes on a colorful job well done.

When you're sitting down to a new color project, the first and most important task is analyzing the job. Objectivity and common sense will help set the tone. If you want to create a powerful impact, you can use a bright color scheme, as shown in the vegetable tray. The stylized pear image shows a more subtle use of color.

Defining Which Colors to Use

Whether you're a beginner or an advanced designer, it's crucial to keep each job in perspective, being mindful of your clients' wishes, budgets, and deadlines. Before diving into any color project, analyze the project on a practical level. Remove yourself from the glitz and glamour of the final product and use common sense as your base. Remember what your client asked for, and then ask yourself the following questions:

1. Who is the audience for this project?

2. What tone does the client want to project?

3. What colors are appropriate for the feel of the project?

4. What is the budget for this project?

5. Is it four color, two color, or is there a fifth color?

6. Does this project require a traditional or modern presence?

7. Is this a selling piece or an informational piece?

8. Will this project require staying power or is it a quick-turn piece?

9. Has the client chosen colors from a sample book?

10. Is this client open to suggestions?

11. Is there money for spot varnish or special paper that will improve color quality?

12. Under what lighting conditions will the final piece be viewed?

Asking these questions is a great way to understand what your client is trying to achieve. Working with color can be fatal to a designer/client relationship if it's not handled with care. This means setting aside preconceived notions and using a commonsense approach.

Warm versus Cool Colors

COLORS ARE PERCEIVED on a cerebral and physical level in many ways and through literally thousands of shades. In the design world, colors are typically divided into groups of warm, cool, and neutral colors. Warm colors are considered to be reds, yellows, and oranges. Cool colors include greens, blues, and purples, while neutrals run the gamut from browns to grays to black. Depending on whom you talk to or what you read, white is considered a neutral color, cool color, or noncolor.

Developing a trained eye will help you better understand warm versus cool colors. It's as easy as driving down the road, noticing the color of each house, and proclaiming it warm, cool, or neutral. The groupings listed above are a general rule. The waters get muddy when you begin mixing percentages to create new colors. At that point, a cool color can quickly become a warm one.

For example, 100 percent magenta is an extremely cool color. Adding percentages of yellow to magenta has a warming effect. Increasing the yellow to 100 percent, and decreasing the magenta by fixed percentages will result in a continuing change in warmth, until you reach the relative coldness of 100 percent yellow.

The primary process colors—cyan, magenta, and yellow—are inherently cool. Adding percentages of one color to the other has an overall warming effect. Adding percentages of yellow to magenta is a perfect example of this phenomenon.

Learning the subtle differences between warm and cool colors will enhance your ability to combine and contrast elements, while also creating a solid color palette. The overall effect of the chrysanthemum image is cool, with bright magenta highlights and midtones. The close-up photo illustrates contrast between the warm reds of the flower petals and the cool yellows of the pollen within.

Color
Combinations

If you're stumped when combining color, take inspiration
from the world around you.
Sometimes, the least likely
colors work in harmony. When
you find combinations that
work well together, add them
to your repertoire.

IF YOU COULD BE ANY COLOR of the
rainbow, what color would you be? Cool
ice blue? Elegant royal purple? Flashy
metallic gold? It may be a silly question,
but it's worth asking as it gives insight
into the type of colors you feel comfortable with and that work well together.

Even color aficionados differ on which
colors are warm or cool or which combinations work best together. Colors
can work in harmony, or they can clash.
Your choices depend on the look you're
striving for and the aura you're hoping
to project.

Beyond the warm and cool designations, colors are typically lumped into
categories such as natural, rich, muted,
and calm. Natural colors are a perfect
definition for the term "subjective."
What you might consider natural,
the next person will deem unnatural.
Natural colors are often associated with
the great outdoors: green grass, blue
sky, brown tree trunks, or orange leaves.
These are terrific no-nonsense colors
that appeal to most individuals and are
a safe bet for designs.

This photograph presents an
interesting combination of
warm browns and cool greens
and reds. The contrast helps to
enhance the poignant impact
of the image. (Photo courtesy
of Audrey Baker.)

Color is Mother Nature's gift to designers, and as luck would have it, glorious greens, blues, oranges, and browns are soothing to even the most discerning eye. In the first set of images, you can see the range of warm color combinations. The second set illustrates the cool combinations found in a single green leaf.

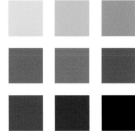

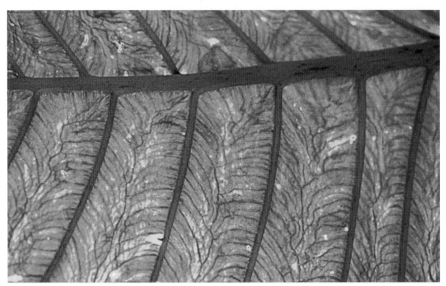

Rich Colors

REDS, PURPLES, ROYAL BLUES, FOREST GREENS, AND BURGUNDIES with deep tones are examples of rich colors. Various percentages of black dictate how dense these colors can be, and how well they will print. The historical colors of royalty, these tones convey depth and weight. They work well in contrast and in combination with highlight color, but you should be careful not to overuse them. A page enveloped in rich color can quickly overwhelm a design. This can reduce the information you are trying to convey, and make the finished piece feel excessively dramatic and overdesigned.

Small percentages of color can make a big difference to the outcome of your project. Relatively minor fluctuations in color density, whether in solid color blocks or a smattering of stones, can make a big difference. These colored blocks illustrate only a 3 percent fluctuation in percentages of cyan, yellow, and magenta. How many variations of gray do you see in the stones?

Muted Colors

MANY DESIGNERS HAVE TROUBLE working with what they consider to be calm or muted colors. Here, instinct and judgment must dictate your color selections, and playing the color percentages comes to the forefront. Percentages of base colors can vary greatly, as neutrals colors are most prone to shifting on press.

If you have a job that requires loads of muted color, your best insurance is to run a test proof with your printer. Set up a page containing different color blocks with different percentages, and it will make your job infinitely easier.

Muted colors can combine to present an effective image and feel. A simple wall can contain dozens of subtle shades from pale yellow to rusty orange to dark brown.

Colors That Make a Statement

CLOSE YOUR EYES and think about what you've seen in the last twenty-four hours. What sticks out in your mind and why? Is it the green pasture you strolled through, the swirling beige coffee you drank this morning, or those blue guys on a television commercial? No matter what you saw or where you saw it, certain colors made an impact. Color has a way of seeping into your brain and staying there, whether it's a Caribbean sunset or a burnt roast.

What makes something memorable? Words, expressions, and color. Just ask anyone in advertising. The same rules apply to design, whether it's in print or on the Web. Depending on your medium and project, the use of bold colors, patterns, and letters can have enormous impact and longevity.

Creations with bold color and unique imagery often become embedded in our memories. Playing with strong colors is fun, but it's easy to cross the line into garish.

Yellow is a key component to many color mixes, and you can easily go overboard with it.

The Yellow Factor

FOR SOME BIZARRE REASON, people are mad for the color yellow. While yellow as a stand-alone color may be too perky for some designers, it is very practical for most media and a crucial element to mixing colors. Designers find that yellow causes much trouble both in proof and final product. It is a key component in many color mixes and it's a tough mix to get right. Whenever you're designing a color job, keep a printed sample of yellow color blocks handy. It's a great reference and reminder of what could happen if yellow is misused.

These blocks give a range of yellow percentages from 20 to 100 in increments of 10 percent. The second set of blocks shows the same increments of yellow with 20 percent cyan added to each.

Opposites Attract
(I.E., THE GREEN/RED FACTOR)

MANY DESIGNERS will argue that colors must be complementary in order to be pleasing to the eye. However, the radical design faction will argue to the death, that contrasting colors are the only way to use color. In this instance, both parties are correct—but it depends solely on the type of project you are working on.

Colors at the opposite end of the spectrum, like red and green, have caused arguments for years. Some people see spots, while others see Christmas. Obviously, colors that are closer together on the color wheel work well together. Colors at opposing ends of the wheel can also work well together if used in the proper context.

Contrasting colors is tricky business, and the more you use them in a single project, the more garish they become. However, when used for a specific purpose, the resulting piece can be wildly successful.

Contrasting colors make a strong statement and can work well together in the proper context. The red/green combination is a common occurrence in nature, but a little goes a long way. The goal is to highlight, not nauseate.

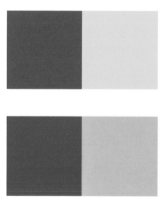

On a traditional color wheel, complementary colors are diametrically opposed. In this case, the combinations are red/green, violet/yellow, and blue/orange.

SUMMARY

BUILDING THE FOUNDATIONS of a solid clientele depends on your knowledge and understanding of color and color combinations. Discovering and sharing the concepts, impact, and possibilities of color can be one of the most rewarding elements of graphic design. As a design professional, it's important to explore the variety of available resources from which you can expand your color repertoire. Graphics handbooks are invaluable tools for ideas, along with books on interior and exterior design, architecture, and landscape design. The natural world can also provide endless inspiration. Visiting wild animal parks and botanical gardens, or even local attractions, with a designer's eye for color can lead you in effective, unusual, and exciting directions.

COLOR CORRECTION, MANIPULATION, AND PROOFING SYSTEMS

YOUR SCREEN IS FILLED WITH COLOR. The images are glorious, perfectly adjusted, and ready for mass consumption. But are they really? Are those "perfect" photographs the real thing, or simply a trick of the eye? You didn't bother running proofs of any of them, why would you if the images appeared to be perfect? If you're a rookie designer, you wouldn't, and that could be a costly mistake. What you see is not what you get, and if you didn't take the time to create and test your color percentages, and didn't run a sample proof, you're in for a very unpleasant surprise.

Color imagery and proofing are kindred spirits. They rely and thrive on one another, and any designer worth their Sharpie pays heed to this all-important relationship. Knowing how to manipulate color is vitally important, and proofing those manipulations is also crucial. If you learn one thing as a designer, it's that color is a fantasy world, and the only way to bring it to reality is to back up your actions with hard evidence.

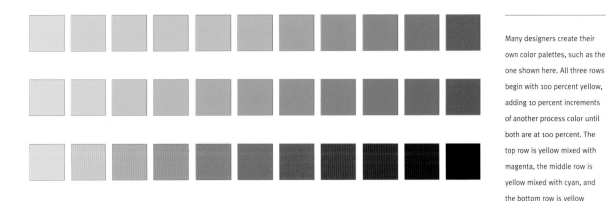

Many designers create their own color palettes, such as the one shown here. All three rows begin with 100 percent yellow, adding 10 percent increments of another process color until both are at 100 percent. The top row is yellow mixed with magenta, the middle row is yellow mixed with cyan, and the bottom row is yellow mixed with black.

Creating a Trusted Color Palette

DESIGNERS LOVE EXPERIMENTING with color because it offers freedom, movement, and creativity. However, those enticements often come at a high price. Before attempting any color-manipulation or color-correction process, it's important to develop a palette of tried-and-tested colors that you feel comfortable with and you know will print superbly.

Learning the nuts and bolts of color means learning how to mix and match colors using percentages. In most graphics software, you can easily create such a palette, saving it for use on future design jobs or tailoring it to specific projects. It's a good idea—and well worth the effort—to experiment with mixed percentages of the four process colors, for example taking 100 percent magenta and adding increments of 10

percent yellow, until you reach red. Then do the same thing with 10 percent increments of cyan and black. This will provide a solid base for any palette, especially as you add new mixes with each new project. Duplicating these mixtures on a single page, and having the printer run a proof, will give you a fabulous archive of color swatches that you can refer to at any time.

You can also add variations of colors you've already created to the palette. For example, if you have a particular shade of teal, you can create a list of percentages for that color beginning at 100 percent and moving down to 10 percent. As you will quickly find out, the combinations are endless.

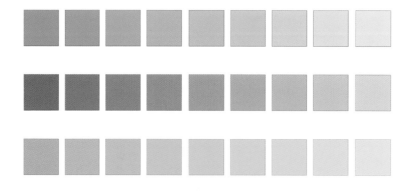

Experimenting with percentages always yields new and exciting combinations. Any premixed color is also fair game for your palette. These rows are examples of already mixed shades reduced in 5 percent increments. The top row starting color is a mix of 72 percent cyan and 38 percent yellow. The middle row starts at 43 percent cyan and 76 percent magenta. The bottom row starts at 56 percent magenta and 87 percent yellow.

This forest pond, with its varying shades of garish yellow and blurry pastel pinks, screams overexposure. Working with the brightness and contrast will help, but in the long run, these images require lots of tinkering with hue, saturation, and density settings.

Color Correction
and Manipulation

MANIPULATING AND CORRECTING
COLOR IMAGES is like dancing with the
devil—you never know when you'll get
burned. As with all color work, the key to
avoiding problems is to manipulate
color percentages, learn the color-
editing functions of your graphics
program, and run a proof with your
printer. Images can suffer from any
number of color maladies, including
oversaturation, over- and underexpo-
sure, extreme shadows and highlights,
subtle color variations, and in many
cases, poor original art.

This image is a perfect example
of oversaturation. The murky
magenta and blue tones overwhelm the image, making it
blurry and hard to adjust.
Adding to the difficulty are
the subtle highlights, deep
shadows, and the blown-out
yellows in the sun.

Everyone loves silhouettes, but they're a nightmare for designers. If you're lucky, manipulating brightness and contrast can do the trick, but most of the time you'll need to heavily manipulate hue and saturation, taking care to prevent the image from becoming murky and plugging up on press.

Saturation

HEAVILY SATURATED IMAGES ARE TRICKY to manipulate. What appears to be a slight adjustment on screen can result in huge differences in the printed product. You can try experimenting with these images, but your best insurance is to create a ganged sample page and have your printer run a test file. Make notes of the modifications performed on each image and then compare them to the proof. Only then can you continue adjusting images with reasonable certainty.

Remember that oversaturated images in the design stage will probably become even more saturated on press due to dot gain. Once on press, the only cure for oversaturated images is to reduce the amount of ink applied to the paper, which can have a negative effect on all of the other elements of your design.

Images with heavy shadows
are equally tough to manipulate, as this poorly constructed
image shows. Working with
shadows takes a lot of practice, as it is very easy to over-
work the shadowy areas and
have them posterize on press.

Subtle color variation is the
ultimate trickster when color
manipulation is required. The
complex browns and yellows in
this image make it extremely
difficult to shift certain portions without shifting others.
As a rule, you should avoid
making radical corrections
and try to retouch only the
glaring problems.

Poor original art is a common
complaint among designers.
This blurry image has bad
exposure, saturation, dust and
scratches, and a moving target.
If you are compelled to fix
such an image, take solace
in knowing that it can't look
much worse.

This image, heavily saturated
with blue and black, is a perfect example of how difficult
manipulations can be. The
original version (top left) is
murky and needs adjustment.
However, the progression of
accompanying images from
top to bottom shows what
happens as you lift cyan in
10 percent increments.

The magenta in this image is
oversaturated to such an
extent that it glows. At first
glance, it's too garish,
but reducing the saturated
magenta by even 10 percent
can turn this image around.
The trick is making sure that
the background blues don't
turn purple.

This original image (above),
though captivating, suffers
from a massive dose of yellow. Manipulating the yellow
is complicated because the
entire image is affected. This
is the type of image you want
to proof, no matter the cost,
because even the slightest
color adjustment will be dramatic. The image at left has
30 percent of the saturated
yellow removed.

Highly overexposed images,
such as this beach shot,
require careful adjustments.
You can modify brightness and
contrast only after increasing
the midtones, in this case, by
approximately 20 percent. The
before and after images are
quite startling.

Over- and Underexposure

AT FIRST GLANCE, MOST OF THESE
images appear unusable, but with the
surge in photo-manipulation technology,
many can be salvaged. In some cases,
you'll get lucky, and a simple brightness
or contrast adjustment will do the trick.
Or you can use the more-sophisticated
Levels or Curves functions in Adobe
Photoshop to independently modify
highlights, shadows, and midtones.
However, with many images, you'll have
to execute multiple manipulations with
all four process colors to achieve the
desired effect.

Underexposed images are common and can be easy to adjust. This image, taken on a cloudy day, is remedied by manipulating the brightness, contrast, and sharpness of the image. Notice how the colors leap from the page.

Extreme Shadows and Highlights

THIS IS WHERE COLOR RETOUCHING gets interesting and frustrating. Images that contain extreme shadows or highlights are problematic, even under the best circumstances. The unfortunate byproduct of dealing with these images is that no two are alike. Shadows are often in danger of becoming posterized, and highlights can become bright white splotches on the image. Practice makes perfect when it comes to retouching these images, and the more you manipulate, the better you'll get at adjusting them for optimal reproduction.

Food photography suffers
from highlight anxiety on a
daily basis. Reflections from
a camera flash wreak havoc
on just about any surface.
These peppers were retouched
by adjusting the brightness
to reduce the white glare
and contrast to even the
color saturation.

When adjusting for shadows, you need to be careful that you're not distorting the entire image. With a photo as dense and shadowy as this, you have to work slowly to adjust the midtones and brightness in small increments.

Shadows on faces are com-
mon, and fixing them is not
always easy. In an image like
this, compromise is the better
part of valor. The original is
muddy and saturated. You
can bring out the warrior's
beautiful expression by using
Adobe Photoshop to modify
brightness and midtones, but
doing so while maintaining
the richness of the blue sky
can be tricky.

Some images that contain
extreme shadow and highlights
cannot be manipulated effectively. In this case, the image
is still effective without any
adjustment.

As you can see in these four comparison photos, a minute adjustment of 5 to 15 percent less magenta can make a significant difference. The first image is the original; the three that follow have respectively had 5, 10, and 15 percent magenta removed.

Subtle Color Variation

OVERADJUSTING IMAGES that contain similar tones and shades can be devastating, because ink densities on the press have a significant effect, and subtle variations that are possible on the computer may not fall within the press's CMYK gamut. Use care when retouching any images with subtle color variation.

No matter what images you're color correcting and manipulating, it's important to send a sample to your printer for proofing. In addition to offering relief from color uncertainty, it will help secure your professionalism in the design field. What follows are the different types of proofs available to you and your client.

Reproduction of skin tones can be controversial and subjective. As illustrated in this series of model photos, skin tones that could be construed as too pink or too yellow if photographed separately prove to be accurate representations of natural color variations when shown together.

Images of food are among
the most demanding projects
for designers. The key to success is excellent photography
that conveys palatability,
freshness, and festivity.
These are examples of good
photographs that need
little overall retouching
or manipulation.

Running proofs early and often is the key to any successful color project. You should always check questionable images; even one that looks reasonably good on screen can have disastrous results on press. This before-and-after representation of an image is a perfect example of why designers should make the proofing process part of their regular routine.

Types of Proofs

PROOFING ON ANY PRINTING PROJECT CAN NEVER BEGIN TOO SOON. "Proof early and proof often" is sound advice and pays dividends in successful press runs. Proofing follows a pattern of succession and can be broken into the following categories:

Design Layout Proofs

THE FIRST PROOFS GENERATED IN PRINT projects are those produced during the conceptual and design stages. It's common here to perform preliminary scanning of critical images for color correction and manipulation. These images are generally sent to color prepress houses or the printer, and serve a dual purpose: They can be grouped on single sheets as printed proofs, and they can be adjusted electronically. Designers who use established color-management systems often bypass hard proofs at this stage, and work directly with electronic scans.

Basic design proofs are generally produced on monochrome laser printers and low-end color printers, with placeholders designated as *position only* (POs) or *for position only* (FPOs), for the high-resolution scans to follow. This stage is rarely used for final color approval.

Screen-Build Proofs

IF YOU PLAN TO USE A CMYK PROCESS to replicate Pantone spot colors, you may be in for an unpleasant surprise. Many Pantone colors can't be accurately translated into four-color process because the gamut of CMYK isn't large enough to replicate the spot-color pigments. For jobs with high expectations, it's worth the expense to send your printer a file with small blocks of screen-built colors for proofing. If the results don't meet your expectations, you'll have time to make adjustments in the early stages of the project before going to the expense of final contract proofs and last-minute changes.

You should also consider the eventual impact of making final color adjustments on press. Adjusting four-color images on press will also affect screen-built spot colors. For example, if the press operator adds more magenta to an image, any colors built with magenta will also show a color shift. If accurate Pantone matching is essential, consider adding it as a fifth spot color.

Screen-build proofs can be a simple series of blocks proofed on a single sheet. This provides a valuable visual reference and allows you to make minor percentage adjustments before committing the project to the final contract proofing stage.

Making on-press color adjustments to four-color images will also affect screen builds. The image on the left is printed with standard process color ink densities. Increasing magenta to enhance the red in the image also increases the red in the screen build.

Four-color images and screen-built color blocks can be ganged together on a preliminary color proof before committing the project to the final proofing stage, where changes and corrections can be costly.

Gang Proofs

SIMILAR TO SCREEN-BUILD PROOFS in intent, gang proofs are scanned and scaled photos of four-color images grouped onto a single sheet for color proofing. For images that may require color retouching and manipulation, this is a cost-effective approach to achieving the final proofing results you're seeking, without the expense of reproofing an entire job with scattered four-color photos. This can also be done in concert with screen-built blocks, and can put you on the right track with screen percentages and color images at the same time.

For jobs with multiple Pantone color-matching criteria, another option is to print the job using the patented six-color process described later in this chapter. This increases the color gamut on press tremendously and provides far more accuracy for screen-build matches.

Ganging images on a preliminary high-resolution proof can
save time and money on corrections at the final proofing
stage. Scanned and scaled
images can be electronically
placed in random order to
best fit the most economical
proof size and then reviewed
for color.

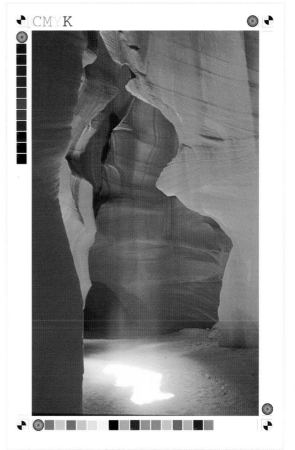

Proofing Systems

systems are an integral part of the evolution of prepress technology. Major manufacturers such as Kodak, Agfa, Fuji, Hewlett-Packard, and Creo are part of the pack, and the range of proofing technologies can be overwhelming. High-resolution proofing is generally quite accurate, and most printers and prepress houses maintain consistent quality standards. All proofing systems are subject to a wide range of variables, and no single proofing system is inherently superior in all respects. Two separate printing houses—using identical proofing systems to produce final proofs of identical electronic files—can produce output that displays significant differences in color and fidelity. These variations are caused by differences in hardware settings, exposures, chemical maintenance, machine maintenance, and handling.

These proofs are examples of the same file processed and proofed by two different printers using the same proofing system. Most printers adjust their proofing system to closely match the capabilities of the printing presses they use.

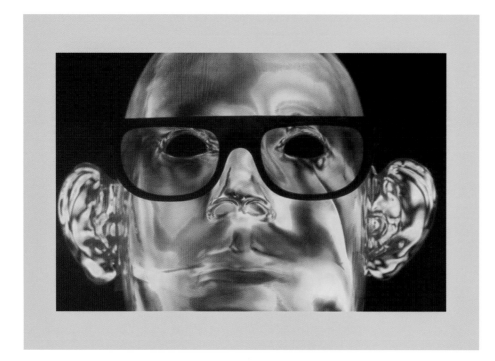

Many proofing systems reproduce Pantone colors as CMYK builds, even if the spot colors are to be printed separately on press. To ensure that the printer is aware of this, you should clearly mark your additional color locations on the proof.

Proofing Purposes and Expectations

Proofs to Your Printer

Remember that if you are unable to run separated proofs from your files, your printer probably won't be able to run separated files either. Supplying separated lasers is critical to ensuring good communication and avoiding costly errors when the job is in the printer's hands. Many printers won't even accept a job if separated lasers aren't included in your submission package. Those that do will often send you a change order for additional costs if they encounter problems.

BEFORE ANY RESPONSIBLE PRINTER puts a job on press, they will expect the client to sign-off on a proof. The purpose of a proof is to represent what will be printed on press, within the predictable limitations of the proofing system. It's important to establish these limitations with your printer as early as possible—preferably before sending the job out (see Chapter 4 for more information on working with your printer). Printers use a variety of systems that can produce proofs with color gamut and brightness that be either less or more than what's possible on press.

Proofing Spot Color

ONE IMPORTANT ELEMENT WITH many proofing systems—and virtually all digital proofing systems—is that spot colors printed separately from the process colors will be proofed either as composite CMYK or as a separate proofing pigment. This may not precisely represent the specific spot color you've chosen. The Chromalin proofing system allows the proofer to mix specific pigments that will match formulated colors with good accuracy, but this can be pricey because it adds considerably to the time and effort required to precisely match pigments. For critical color matching and client approval, the cost can be justified. The key to saving money and time is to clearly identify your color breaks and, if possible, mark them on the proofs you receive so that all parties will be aware of each spot color's placement. To ensure that there are no surprises on press, you need to communicate your specifications and run your own separated laser proofs.

Separated Proofs

Along with electronic files, you should supply your printer with separated laser proofs. This ensures that the printer is aware of each color to be printed, and shows that your separations were accurate before they left your possession. Shown here is a four-color job with a fifth color in addition to the black, cyan, magenta, and yellow.

OPEN MONDAY-SATURDAY
STARTING JUNE 31!

Reviewing proofs is the touchstone for any design job. A simple error, such as an incorrect date on a poster, can have costly results. What may seem on the outset to be an easy fix can cost you and your client a new set of color plates, a new makeready, and a missed deadline.

Reviewing Proofs

REVIEWING PROOFS IS EASILY ONE OF THE MOST CRITICAL STAGES for ensuring a high-quality final color product. Once you've signed off on a proof, your printer has every right to assume that the job is okay to print, and the last thing you want to say during a press check is, "Oops, I missed that on the proof." This is particularly dangerous when your client has enough confidence in you to okay the proof without their involvement, as is often the case with reruns that involve only minor changes. Missing the most mundane color alterations, such as a changed date in the small print, can turn an expensive project into an even more-expensive disaster. While printers occasionally complain about clients who are "red pencil happy," they are not responsible for client errors that don't get caught.

Light booths with color-corrected light sources (5,000 degrees Kelvin) present the most accurate and repeatable conditions for reviewing color proofs. This is true in your review of color proofs and at the time your job goes to press. (Courtesy Heidelberg USA, Inc.)

65
...

Color
Correction

Lighting and Proofing

PROPER LIGHTING CONDITIONS are important for proofing and reviewing critical color matches. Viewing booths with 5,000 degree Kelvin corrected light-bulbs are an industry standard, and provide lighting that has the least effect on color appearance. Proofs viewed under fluorescent or incandescent lighting will reflect the cooler colors of fluorescence, or the warmer colors of incandescence.

Lighting and the Pressroom

ANOTHER ELEMENT TO BEAR in mind when analyzing color under various lighting conditions is that most press-room viewing tables are also fitted with color-corrected, 5,000-degree Kelvin lights. The color you see when reviewing proofs under controlled lighting conditions will be the same color you see when your job is on press.

In this example, the original photograph (top) and the proof viewed under fluorescent lighting (bottom) show significant color variation. The differences are due to the ambient light in combination with variations in the dyes and substrates used to make the prints.

Metameric Influence on Proofing

COMPARING COLOR PROOFS TO PHOTO-GRAPHIC PRINTS under uncorrected lighting conditions can show the effects of metamerism. If ambient light alters the color you are viewing, other variables can exacerbate the differences. Dyes used in different proofing systems are not identical, nor are the proofing substrates. Dyes and finishes on photographs also vary depending on the manufacturer. A proof and an original photograph can appear to be closely matched under corrected lighting, while quite dissimilar under other artificial lighting. By the same token, it's possible for a proof and. photograph to display a good color match under fluorescent light and display a significant color shift under corrected lighting. Viewing color proofs under corrected lighting is the only accurate and repeatable method of assessing them.

The same images seen in the
color-corrected light of a
viewing booth show the proof
to be an accurate representation of the photograph. The
light source minimizes color
influence, providing the most
accurate and repeatable environment for good color analysis.

Come
Sail
Away

The Oregon Coast is a place
like no other. Whether
engulfed in fog or blazing
sun, the people and places
are as unforgettable as the
last sunset.

Fishermen claim that Mother
Nature owns the land, but
their mistress is the sea. That is,
perhaps, never more evident
than on the Oregon Coast, a
glorious stretch of land carved
by everchanging time and tide.

On sunny days, its craggy outcrops and sandy shores are kissed by succulent waves. When consumed by fog, the land is reminiscent of coastal Maine, the vague sillouettes of boats fading into the mist like ghostly pirate vessels hunting the high seas.

The quaint coastal villages of the Oregon coast are born of the sea and the local color, both of which are in abundance. The everpresent crash of waves against is in sharp contrast to the sounds of technology so evident in big cities. In towns ranging from Coos Bay to Astoria, the folks one meets are neither opportunists or escapists. They are coastal and they spawn from all walks of life, joining together to celebrate their love for the ocean and all that it represents.

Fisherman spin their yarns faster than a Sunday coffee klatch. Some fish for profit, some for sport, but all will tell that their love for the sea is rooted in respect for the everchanging watery landscape and all that it provides.

Page proofs show content and elements from the designer with position-only placeholders for the four-color process images to be added during the prepress stage. Always make the FPO notation big and easy to identify, so you avoid the risk of printing the low-resolution file.

Page Proofs

PAGE PROOFS ARE FULLY COMPOSED proofs of each page, with all design elements in place. Four-color images can be shown as position-only placeholders in a single color to signify that the final images will be placed at the prepress stage. Page proofs are commonly shown to the client in single pages or as *reader spreads*, which indicate the page sequence of the final job.

Imposition Proofs

YOUR PRINTER CREATES IMPOSITION PROOFS from processed files. These show all of the images and elements as they will appear on the press sheet, and are often folded, collated, stitched, and trimmed to final size to represent the finished product. Imposition proofs show position, content, and color breaks.

Bluelines can be exposed incrementally to show color breaks, but they should be clearly marked to avoid confusion. Some printers will mark up color breaks on bluelines before showing them to you. Others will not take responsibility for this step. When they don't, it's up to you.

Fishermen claim that Mother Nature owns the land, but their mistress is the sea. That is, perhaps, never more evident than on the Oregon Coast, a glorious stretch of land carved by everchanging time and tide.

On sunny days, its craggy outcrops and sandy shores are kissed by succulent waves. When consumed by fog, the land is reminiscent of coastal Maine, the vague sillouettes of boats fading into the mist like ghostly pirate vessels hunting the high seas.

The quaint coastal villages of the Oregon coast are born of the sea and the local color, both of which are in abundance. The everpresent crash of waves against is in sharp contrast to the sounds of technology so evident in big cities. In towns ranging from Coos Bay to Astoria, the folks one meets are neither opportunists or escapists. They are coastal and they spawn from all walks of life, joining together to celebrate their love for the ocean and all that it represents.

Fisherman spin their yarns faster than a Sunday coffee klatch. Some fish for profit, some for sport, but all will tell that their love for the sea is rooted in respect for the everchanging watery landscape and all that it provides.

Bluelines

Bluelines are used as imposition proofs and are often employed as final proofs for simple one- and two-color jobs. As the name implies, these proofs are manufactured with a blue toner that becomes progressively darker with increased exposure to intense light in a vacuum frame. They are exposed using the same film that will be used for producing the press plates. Color breaks can be shown effectively by reducing exposure times, which results in a lighter shade of blue. One caveat here is that the lighter shades of blue representing a lighter color in a two-color job will often look similar to screens printed in the darker color. If these bluelines will be used as final proofs before a press run, it's always a good idea to clearly mark the color breaks. Blueline proofs will also discolor rapidly when exposed to direct sunlight, so care should be taken when transporting them.

Digital Imposition Proofs

Digital imposition proofs are usually made in conjunction with direct-to-press systems and have come a long way in fidelity and color. While still far from being final-proof quality, these imposition proofs offer a four-color continuous-tone representation of the elements that will be imaged onto plates. These proofs are imaged on both sides directly from the prepress system and will accurately portray color breaks.

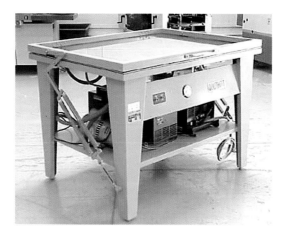

Analog proofs are created using film and proofing material in a vacuum exposure frame similar to this one. These proofs are still common and many believe they offer the most accurate color representation. However, accurate digital proofing systems are quickly becoming more prevalent.

Contract Proofs

AS THE TERM IMPLIES, signing off on a *contract proof* is the indication of an agreement between the client and the printer that the proof will represent the result of the project on press—within the predictable limitations of the proofing system. Contract proofing systems fall into two categories: Analog and digital.

Analog Proofing

ANALOG PROOFS are still common, although they are fading in importance as fully digitized systems become more accessible. This proofing system requires the use of film in a vacuum frame for exposure, one color at a time. These proofs represent the same halftone dot structures that will be produced on the plates. Analog proofing systems have long been considered to be the most accurate of all proofing systems—a notion that is coming under fire as digital proofing becomes more sophisticated.

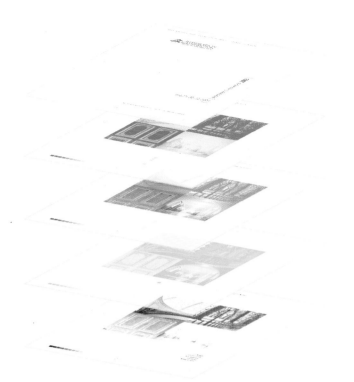

Film Overlay Proofs

Film overlay proofs, often referred to by the 3M trademarked name *Color Key*, have been with us for decades and produce proofs in loose layers that require wet chemical processing. These were part of the analog proofing system before the term was even coined. Film overlay proofs are exposed in a vacuum frame with a single pigmented color representing each of the process colors, then chemically developed, assembled, and taped to a substrate in the manufacturer's predetermined sequence.

With each of the process color pigments fused to an acetate base and the acetates loosely overlayed, a certain amount of air is trapped between each layer. The combination gives the final proof a hazy, grayish cast. This layering and air trapping also allows light to bounce within the layers, creating a *softer* looking dot that is most noticeable in highlights.

Film overlay proofs are the least expensive of the analog proofing systems. A benefit to the system is that additional colors can be added to represent specially formulated ink mixes. While these don't accurately depict each color, the layers can be lifted to ensure accurate color breaks. Many printers still use film overlay proofs, which will probably hold a share of the analog-proofing marketplace for years to come.

Film overlay proofs are loose layers of analog proofing material assembled in predetermined sequences and usually attached on one edge to the substrate. This image shows the progression of black, magenta, cyan, and yellow, and the final results.

CMYK

Occasionally, film overlay proofs are assembled out of sequence, resulting in a slight shift in the final color. Most printers strive to maintain proper sequence, but this is not an uncommon mistake. As you can see, the same image with colors out of sequence shows a significant difference in the final proof.

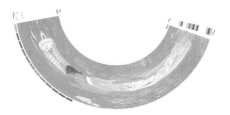

Laminate proofs should be clean, with registration targets and color bars in place. These images show the manufacturer's recommended sequence of yellow, magenta, cyan, and black.

Laminated Proofs

Laminated proofs, which have largely displaced film overlay proofs, were first developed with wet chemical processors, but are now produced with a dry proofing process that does not require use of chemicals or processors. This proofing system is still assembled one color at a time on a single substrate or carrier. Some of these proofing systems allow for a sheet of the actual job stock to be used as the proofing surface. The layers of wet chemical and dry proofing systems are laminated to the substrate in specific sequences (yellow, magenta, cyan, and black). These sequences are determined by the manufacturer, and strict adherence is required to ensure proper color. Occasionally, proofs are accidentally assembled out of sequence, which may result in mild to radical shifts in color.

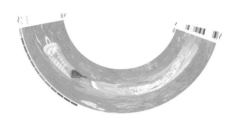

Laminate proofs are some-
times inadvertently assembled
out of sequence. This can
result in a noticeable color
shift that will adversely affect
the balance of color. This is
difficult to detect because the
proofing layers are laminated
tightly together, but the
overlapping color bars will
likely show their own slight
color shift.

Common Denominators of Analog Proofs

All of these systems depend on accurate film assembly and the careful attention of the proofing operator. For years, the people who exposed and processed proofs also burned and developed the plates for the press. Minor slips in these processes, either on the part of the *stripper* who assembles the film layers, or the proofer who assembles the proofs, can result in images out of register on the proof. One common problem with the analog system is damage to the emulsion side of a color. This is often seen in the form of white specks, or holes that appear in that color after the proof is assembled. The emulsion side of any proofing material is highly sensitive, and susceptible to scratches during the assembly process.

Proofs can occasionally slip in the vacuum exposure frame, causing slight but noticeable registration problems. These problems are usually caught and corrected before presentation to the client, but the occasional out-of-register proof can still slip through. If images look out of register, check the targets, and always ask for a revised proof. In this image, you can clearly see that the cyan is out of register.

Areas of pigmented proofing material can flake off during processing, resulting in pinholes and gaps in the final proof. In this example, the magenta pigment was damaged, which can be difficult to detect on the proof before assembly. While this may not represent flaws in the film or affect final printing, these mistakes should be corrected and a new proof, as illustrated on the right, should be supplied.

The *emulsion* side of proofs that carries the process color pigment is quite sensitive, and is sometimes scratched during processing and handling. In this example, the cyan proofing material was accidentally scratched on the left side with a rough fingernail. Remaking the proof, as illustrated in the third image, is the best way to ensure that there are no problems with the film.

In some cases, proofing artifacts result not from the proofing material itself but from scratches on the film that generates the proofs. This is usually noticeable because the scratches allow light to pass through the film and are thus exposed on the proofing medium. In this example, the film used for the cyan plate has been damaged. The only recourse is to reproduce the cyan film and remake the proof.

A common problem with analog proofing systems is contamination by minute dust particles trapped between the film layer and the proof surface. These particles interfere with the contact of film and proof, creating a ring-shaped distortion in dot size and dot pattern. Called *halation*, this usually occurs only in the particular color being exposed, and can be difficult to interpret. Fortunately, the solution is usually simple and experienced prepress professionals will eliminate the problem by examining the film and wiping it clean of debris.

Digital Proofing

COMPUTERIZED DIRECT-TO-PLATE technology is coming on strong. Just as computer-to-film systems eliminated the need for the much slower flatbed cameras of years past, direct-to-plate systems have eliminated the need for film. One factor hindering the acceptance of direct-to-plate has been the lack of adequate proofing systems. Plates are processed for printing only one color each. This means the hardware and software for plate production is designed to handle the digital information and accuracy of a single color. The production of four-color digital proofs presents essentially four times the technical difficulty. Although the pigments and substrates of digital proofing systems are not identical to ink pigments and paper substrates, recent technological advances have resulted in digital proofs that can be matched with remarkable accuracy.

Foreign particles trapped between layers of analog proofs when exposed in a vacuum frame can cause halation, shown by a small ring of distorted dot patterns in the final proof. These are sometimes overlooked at the proofing stage and are one reason why you should inspect proofs carefully.

Earlier digital proofing systems produced representations of the final output, which allowed content proofing, but didn't present a truly accurate medium for color. Current digital systems for contract proofs produce *dot-for-dot* proofs that—like analog proofing systems—provide an accurate representation of the data that will be imaged to the plates. These images are typical examples of what you can expect from modern digital proofing and direct-to-plate printing.

Proofing Systems and Press Operations— Running the Gamut

ANALOG PROOFING SYSTEMS can produce a gamut of approximately six thousand colors, about half again the gamut achievable in offset printing. The simplest explanation for this is that analog proofing systems are manufactured with dyes bonded to plastic surfaces that produce a brighter, purer reflection of CMYK than do printing inks and the substrates that they are applied to. Modern digital proofing systems offer a color gamut of about four thousand—very close to that of high-quality four-color offset printing.

SUMMARY

THERE ARE A NUMBER OF PROOFING
systems used in color reproduction that
provide dependable representations of
color design. Developing a trusted color
palette that can be proofed and reproduced with predictable results will
increase your faith in color choices.
Familiarizing yourself with the proofing
systems that are used for your color
design work, and sharing that knowedge
and experience is invaluable for establishing confidence and building long-
term relationships with your clientele.

COLOR IN PRINT: GETTING THE RESULTS YOU WANT

The three primary process printing colors are cyan, magenta, and yellow. A separate black plate produces a truer black than the relatively muddy combination of CMY and allows for reproduction of detail that the combined colors cannot match. (From left to right: 100C, 100M, 100Y, 100CMY, and 100K.)

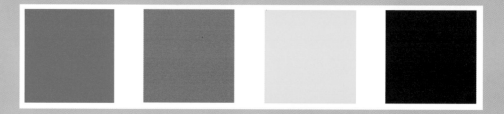

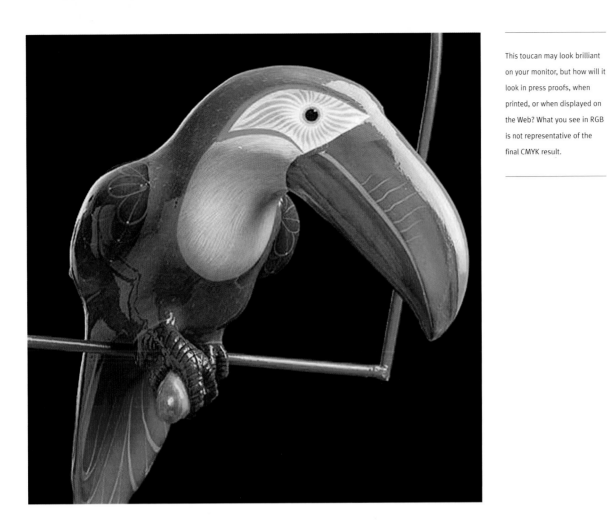

But That's Not the Way It Looks on My Monitor

ACCURATE COLOR REPRODUCTION IS one of the primary goals of printing technology. It can achieve this goal, in part, because the human eye is relatively easy to fool with the right props. Think of really good color printing as one of the most exhaustive and expensive illusions ever created. For all of their flair and dizzying props, Siegfried and Roy can't hold a penlight to the printing industry's achievement in convincing us that the colors we see on the printed page are as real as those created in the natural world.

The color you see on your monitor or television is inherently different from color reproduced in print. Your color monitor emits light by firing electron guns at phosphors embedded in the screen in the primary colors of red, green, and blue (RGB). At full intensity, these three colors combine to produce white. The absence of RGB produces what appears to be black. With myriad variations of RGB, we can produce the array of colors available on today's color monitors.

In the natural world, the primary colors of red, green, and blue (RGB) interact with one another in unlimited combinations. This simplified illustration represents the effect of the primary colors at maximum intensity. All three colors combine at full strength to produce white.

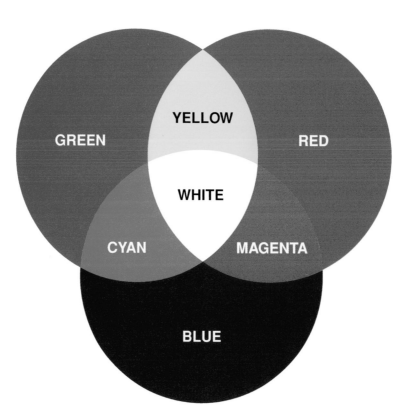

Although this photo is reproduced in CMYK, the images on the monitor will always be RGB. RGB is known as additive color; CMY is referred to as subtractive color, and represents the secondary colors of RGB. CMY combines to produce black, but most printing processes add a black (K) plate for better-quality reproduction.

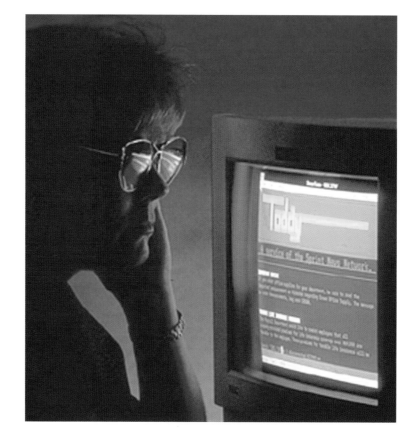

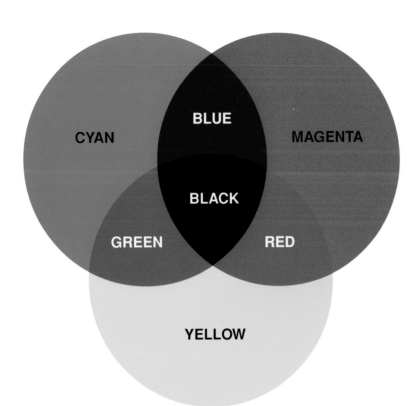

Reflective CMY colors are shown here at 100 percent, separately and in simple combinations. All three colors at this level produce black, but the printing process is best served by a separate black plate.

Secondary RGB Colors—
OUR BELOVED CMY(K)

Additive Color

THE RGB PRIMARY COLORS produced by monitors are commonly known as *additive colors*. The *secondary colors* of RGB—produced by mixing any two primary colors and excluding the third —are cyan, magenta, and yellow. For example, green and blue produce cyan, red and blue result in magenta, and green and red produce yellow. By varying the intensity of RGB, we can run through the gamut of colors available— within the constraints of the monitor— until the eventual result is the strongest color possible: white.

The beauty of RGB is that it closely relates to how we perceive color in the natural world. However, while it is the basis for media that project color, such as your computer monitor and television set, it is useless in print reproduction, which employs CMYK *subtractive* colors. Conversely, no matter how often you convert a design on your computer system to CMYK, it will always be RGB on your screen.

Secondary Colors Turn
the Tables in Print

IN PRINTING REPRODUCTION, the secondary RGB colors—CMY—take the lead, reducing RGB to simple reds, greens, and blues. In print, the combination of magenta and yellow produce red; yellow and cyan result in green; and cyan and magenta combine to give us blue. While the three primary printing colors produce black, this combination alone lacks the snap and detail of a separately applied black ink. Because of this, the print industry has added black (K) to the primary subtractive color lineup. Think of it as the Special Forces member of the CMYK printing process, with several obvious missions and a surprising number of covert talents.

Black ink for commercial printing is manufactured in a variety of pigmented compositions. Process black, which is used in four-color process printing, is a relatively neutral color and is pigmented so that it doesn't shift the hues of the other three primary colors. Most ink manufacturers also produce intense blacks for black-and-white printing. These generally contain blue toners that help produce a colder, stronger black.

Most of the detail in this image is carried by the black printing unit as illustrated in the black-only image. Process black is neutrally pigmented so as not to alter the subtle color variations created by the three primary printing colors of cyan, magenta, and yellow.

Color
in Print

Process black is relatively neutral. Black inks designed for black-and-white printing often contain blue toners that add intensity and "pop," as illustrated by the box on the right.

The modern multicolor printing press is a combination of mechanical units designed to print process colors in rapid succession. The four towers of this sheetfed press contain the inking system, plates, and cylinders for each printing unit. (Courtesy Heidelberg USA, Inc.)

Subtractive Color

SUBTRACTIVE COLOR REFERS TO COLOR in most of our natural world, and in print production. Whereas RGB colors are projected directly from the monitor, CMYK pigments in printing ink absorb ambient light, reflecting the results back to your eyes. The reflection's accuracy depends on the light sources in the immediate environment. Understanding these light sources is key to understanding good color reproduction and, most importantly, to making good color decisions. We will discuss the full effect of light in greater detail in Chapter 5.

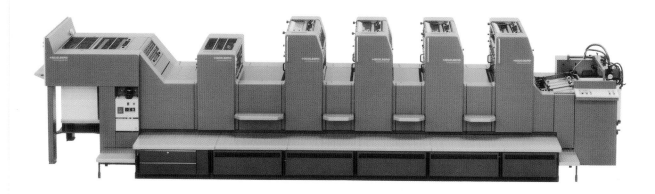

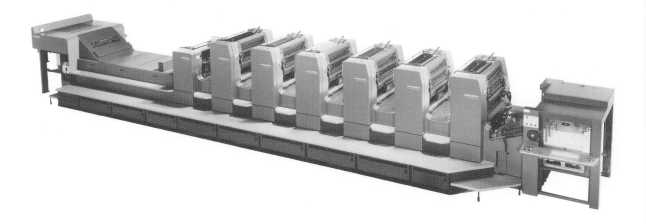

The Color Printing Process One Step at a Time

Today's four-color printing process requires consistent color sequences. This printing press is running with black ink in the first printing unit, cyan in the second, magenta in the third, and yellow in the fourth. The fifth and sixth units can be used for printing spot varnishes or specially mixed additional colors. (Courtesy Heidelberg USA, Inc.).

AS A GRAPHIC DESIGNER, it pays for you to have a basic understanding of how color is printed. With this knowledge, you'll be able to better mix and match colors, make repairs, and avoid potential disasters. A little press knowledge goes a long way toward putting you ahead of the competition.

In four-color print production, cyan, magenta, yellow, and black inks are applied to the paper in microscopically thin layers. With modern multicolor printing presses, these applications of ink occur in rapid succession. Printers establish and maintain strict sequences for printing each of the colors. The color sequence is important for several practical and economic reasons. Modern printing presses can operate at incredible speeds, requiring many related systems to function nearly perfectly in the blink of an eye. Many printers use a standardized printing sequence of black ink in the first printing unit, cyan ink in the second, magenta in the third, and yellow in the fourth. When producing projects with a great deal of black ink coverage, the black ink will often be moved from the first printing unit (*first*

down black) to the fourth printing unit (*fourth down black*). We're not talking about football strategies, but the decisions can be equally important to producing the desired results.

Whether sheetfed or web, the offset press is the standard for high-quality and economical four-color printing. Understanding the process in a real-world setting is a key to achieving your desired results. For the following example, we'll focus on commercial sheetfed multicolor offset presses.

The moment the operator pushes the Feed Paper and Print buttons, a sheet of paper begins a swift and complicated journey. When entering the first printing unit, the sheet is pulled between two rotating cylinders. On the surface of one cylinder is a rubberized blanket covered with a thin coat of ink representing a reversed duplicate of the image on the printing plate. This image is delicately pressed onto the paper's surface as it passes through the cylinders under highly calculated and consistent pressures.

In this standard printing sequence, black is the first color printed and has the highest tack, or stickiness, of the four process colors, allowing the subsequent inks to stick to it with optimum dot fidelity.

The second color in sequence is cyan, with a slightly lower tack, printing over the black.

The third color is magenta, with less tack than cyan, printing over both black and cyan.

Yellow has the lowest tack, and is printed over the black, cyan, and magenta. Lower tack allows the ink to print smoothly over the three previous colors. It also causes more dot gain, which is largely unnoticed. The four process colors are now combined, one after the other, in the blink of an eye, to create the final process-color image.

Properties of Printing Ink for the Technically Disinterested

JUST LIKE THE PAINT you use on your bathroom walls, ink combines a pigment with a base *vehicle* that allows the press operator to move the pigment from the ink can to the press ink fountain, inking rollers, plate, rubber blanket, and finally to paper. Once on the paper, the vehicle's job is done and it's time to get rid of it. Ink contains additives that enhance elimination of the vehicle through evaporation and absorption into the paper, along with additives that harden and dry the pigments as they rest on the paper's surface.

Beyond the pigment color, several other differences distinguish the four process-color inks. The first ink to be printed is the stickiest. This stickiness is referred to as *tack* and plays a significant role in the successful, reasonably accurate application of the subsequent colors. It's much like a peanut butter and jelly sandwich. You probably apply the peanut butter first, then the jelly. Peanut butter sticks to the bread, and the jelly sticks to the peanut butter. Try it the other way around, and you wind up with jelly on the bread, and peanut butter all over the place.

We're as consistent with our sandwich assemblies as printers are with their ink sequences. Each ink applied to the paper is successively less sticky. Almost universally, yellow has the lowest tack, and is the last primary color to be printed. Understanding the reason for this also helps explain some of the inherent difficulties of in-line multicolor printing.

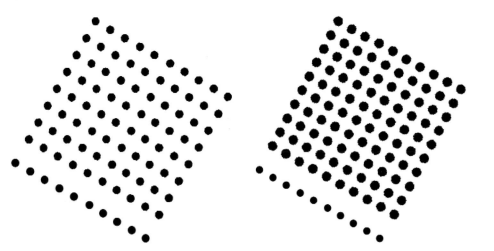

The fibers in uncoated paper absorb and spread ink pigments. On the lower left is an enlargement of hypothetically perfect 20 percent dots. On the right, the same dots are printed on uncoated paper with a significant increase in dot gain.

A Dot's Gain
Is Our Loss

SUCCESSIVELY LOWER TACKS IN PRINTING INKS cause successively greater problems in printing dots with optimal detail. The stickier the ink, the better its ability to maintain the dimensions of dots on the printing plates. Lower ink tack increases dot size, as the less-sticky edges of the dots tend to flow outward. This phenomenon is commonly referred to as *dot gain*.

Dot gain is a fact of life for printers, and controlling it is a key challenge. Sophisticated printers even consider it in their proofing processes, building dot gain into their proofs. They manage dot gain by applying industry standards and thoroughly testing their own systems.

Uncoated paper causes much more dot gain than coated paper. This is because its spongy surface fibers absorb ink outward from the dot's edges to a greater degree. You should avoid screen frequencies greater than 133 lines per inch on uncoated papers because the dots tend to run together. In this case, a high screen value doesn't necessarily result in greater detail. On uncoated papers, you can significantly increase detail simply by decreasing screen values, such as from 175 lines per inch to 133 lines per inch.

A composite proof, as shown here, can match what was expected when the job went to press.

Excessive dot gain, as illustrated here, can cause a muddy, oversaturated effect. Too much ink and/or improperly adjusted printing pressures can increase dot gain to an unacceptable level.

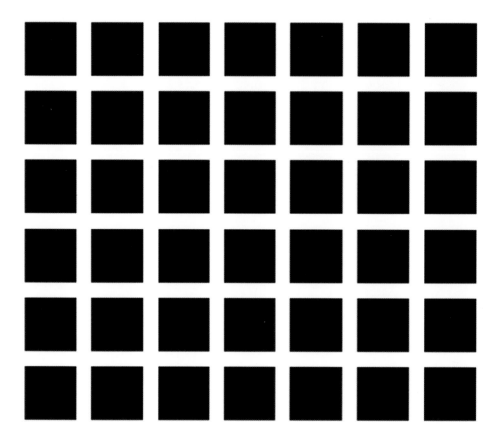

The gray images you see between the corners of these squares illustrate optical dot gain. Optical dot gain creates the illusion of a ghost image on the paper.

Optical Dot Gain

DOT GAIN ALSO HAS AN ILLUSORY aspect, called *optical dot gain*, which causes us to see faint shadow images. This results, in part, from minute shadows being cast onto the surface of the paper from printed dots. Another factor is light passing through the paper's surface and reflecting back from minute amounts of ink that have soaked into the sheet. The eye perceives this as an overall increase in density on the printed sheet.

The Challenge
of Yellow

BECAUSE YELLOW IS SUCH A LIGHT color, its effect on color images is based more on saturation and density than on carrying fine detail. Even with a printer's loupe, it's difficult to see a ten percent yellow dot, even though the same dot sizes can be quite visible in any of the other process colors. As a result, the yellow printing unit is the least affected by the dot gain caused by low tack. One challenge in keeping the yellow unit printing reasonably well isn't so much in maintaining detail as it is in keeping the yellow dots from completely filling in. A dot gain of as much as 50 percent is not uncommon with low-tack yellow ink in the fourth printing unit.

Dot gain is a fluctuating phenomenon that varies from
press to press and color to
color. Because yellow is nor-
mally printed at the end of the
color sequence, the gain in dot
size is greater than it is with
the other process colors. It's
also the least harmed by
significant dot gain. The
yellow in these images convey
color and saturation without
the necessity of carrying
fine detail.

Ink Density

ANOTHER POWERFUL INFLUENCE on dot gain is the amount of ink applied to each sheet of paper, a factor known as *ink density*. Fortunately, this is a measurable quantity, and it is generally kept within predetermined optimal ranges. We can make most of our fine-tuning color adjustments within this range, and achieve wide variations in the final color. Ink manufacturers mix as much pigment as is reasonably possible into all of their colors and try to formulate strong colored inks without compromising the handling characteristics that are necessary to get the ink onto the paper in the first place.

Pushing the upper limits of ink density can produce brighter, more vibrant color. Increased color density also tends to produce a warmer overall color effect. However, it also increases dot gain and can result in oversaturation and loss of detail. With the right printing project, some images can benefit from increased brightness and warmth and won't being excessively harmed by loss of detail. In this case, little damage is done by pushing the limits. We often encourage clients and press operators to crank it up. This usually sends the latter into a cold sweat, but with proper attention and care, it can produce spectacular results.

The drawbacks of pushing ink density include increased drying time — the bane of print estimators and pressroom managers — and the potential transfer or *setting off* of ink onto the backside of overlying sheets in the delivery pile. Again, with attention to detail, these risks are often well worth the extra effort.

The other end of the density range is running the ink *spare*. This can be practical in projects that have been poorly scanned, or those that require a high level of detail. Lighter ink density tends to make the ink stickier on the printing plates and blankets, enabling greater dot fidelity. Lower ink densities also create cooler color schemes.

The downside is that increased stickiness tends to tear coatings and fibers from the paper's surface. This can cause a speckled look, while contaminating the press's inking system with paper particles that often come back to haunt us in the form of *hickeys*. A hickey is an inked image of a particle surrounded by a white halo. The halo appears because the particle blocks ink transfer to the blanket.

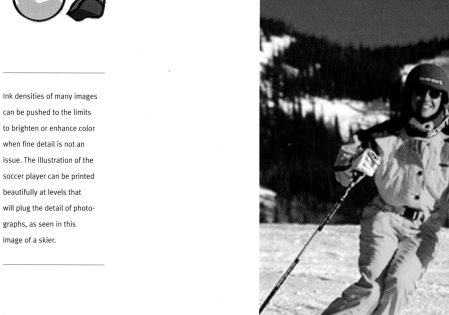

Ink densities of many images can be pushed to the limits to brighten or enhance color when fine detail is not an issue. The illustration of the soccer player can be printed beautifully at levels that will plug the detail of photographs, as seen in this image of a skier.

Lowering ink density can reduce dot gain and increase detail. This can be a quick fix to the expensive alternative of pulling the job for color correction. A better approach is to anticipate dot gain on dense images and make corrections at the proofing stage.

99
...

Color
in Print

Additives on Press

THE PRESS OPERATOR CAN ADDRESS some of these drawbacks by adding a softening agent to the ink fountains, which reduces the tack to more acceptable levels. Another approach is to add some neutral ink base to the ink fountains, which lightens the color while allowing the press operator to run sufficient ink densities to prevent tearing the paper coating. Running ink too lightly almost invariably results in a washed-out appearance. It's generally unwise to run ink too lightly on any printing job, but the practice has a place in the highly subjective color process.

A primary reason for maintaining the same printing sequence is consistency and predictable results. While process printing inks are generally thought to be transparent, the sequence of printing each layer of ink has a noticeable affect on the final appearance of the printed sheet. Printing in a consistent sequence of black, cyan, magenta, and yellow will produce similar results, time after time. If we were to switch the sequence to black, then magenta, cyan, and yellow, the finished result would be visually different, even with identical ink densities. One reason is that our ink tacks are formulated for a consistent sequence. By switching ink sequence, we've also switched our ink tack requirements, and we're back to spreading peanut butter onto jelly.

100
...

**GRAPHIC
DESIGNER'S
COLOR
HANDBOOK**

Subtle changes in ink densities of cyan, yellow, and magenta can be made on press to achieve pleasing color balances. However, press operators and press-room managers will happily explain the ramifications of pushing the limits too far. Here, the printer added yellow to the first image and magenta to the second. The third image is printed with standard overall ink density. The correct color is subjective.

Color Balance

MANAGING COLOR BALANCES—while remaining within reasonable ink density ranges—is much like driving on a freeway. You can drift a bit to the left or a bit to the right with relative impunity, but start crossing the lines and you can get into trouble. Trust your printer on the locations of the lines. They've probably encountered every problem imaginable by crossing them too far, and a good printer won't let you do it.

The reality of color printing is that successive ink applications on in-line multi-color presses reduce print quality and fidelity. The challenge for today's printer is to keep the losses in dot accuracy to a minimum and experienced printers do a remarkably good job of it.

102
...

GRAPHIC
DESIGNER'S
COLOR
HANDBOOK

Paper:
THE MEDIUM AND
THE PRICE YOU PAY

Sheetfed presses are designed
to print *cut sheets*—paper
manufactured in rolls and
then trimmed on guillotine
cutting machines to specific
parent sizes.

PAPER IS THE BASIC MEDIUM FOR COMMERCIAL PRINTING applications and the variety of stock available is staggering. Paper can be the most expensive element of printing projects. Prepress costs on most projects are generally stable and consistent from job to job, but the length of the press run and choice of paper have the most influence on production costs. Successful printers work hard to establish ongoing relationships with paper vendors, and these relationships can translate into significant savings for the print buyer. All other elements being equal, the printer who can negotiate the best paper prices will also give you the best prices. Because paper is an outsource purchase for the printer, you will always be paying for a markup. This can range from 10 to 30 percent, and is usually a moving target. Most of the time, printers who know they are competing for a particular project will revisit the markup on the paper as a first step in lowering prices. When the very best quality is desired and the customer's budget is not limited, premium-quality paper is always the best choice. For situations where the budget is more sensitive, considering a comparable stock in a lower grade may be the best option. Print reps can be very helpful in offering suggestions, and good printers can work wonders with less expensive papers.

Web paper rolls can be huge, standing 3 to 5 feet high and weighing thousands of pounds. Fork trucks with pole attachments maneuver rolls into position for feeding through the presses.

Paper Availability: The "Here Today, Gone Tomorrow" Trap

PAPER LINES COME AND GO AS QUICKLY as automobile styles, and the paper swatches you got from your vendor a year ago may be unavailable today. Paper manufacturers often unleash a wave of hip new paper finishes and colors, only to have them fall flat in the marketplace. It's common to see graphic designers who have created an entire image package based on a new hypothetical paper line like "Extravaganza Marquis" in the "Bubble-wrap" finish and "Twinkletoes" shade. A few phone calls later, and guess what? It's available, but not in that shade; the stock is available in cut sheets, but no one has envelopes; or the entire line has been discontinued.

Paper manufacturing is a competitive industry, driven by the basic laws of supply and demand. A hot new paper that is well received by the design community can generate tremendous revenue for the manufacturer. New offerings are produced in limited supply on a regular basis, and many new paper lines don't trigger much positive response. Without demand, there's no point in producing a supply that will sit on the warehouse floor.

Web presses feed paper through the press from a continuous roll of stock. Paper is trimmed and folded to size after it is printed.

Taking Stock

If your budget is tight, consider lowering your choice of stock grades before dropping design elements. Beautiful printing is done every day on number two and number three grade stocks. A good design produced by a good printer will look terrific, and few will be the wiser. One of the most memorable images ever printed, an Afghan girl in *National Geographic*, was printed on a number three grade coated sheet.

You should always double check with your print rep before committing to any paper with a special finish, color, or an obscure source. You'll save much time, grief, and last-minute scrambling for substitutions by verifying that the paper you have in mind is sitting on a vendor's shelf—preferably with your name on it.

Another consideration is the longevity of a paper line. Even though a paper line may be available right now, it may not be around at all in six months. This can present a problem if you're working on a project that may take several months to get to press. For projects that are unlikely to be reprinted, this doesn't create much of a concern. On the other hand, if your client anticipates regular reprints that will require matching stock, your safest bet is to stick with the tried-and-true stocks, of which there are myriad excellent choices from a wide variety of excellent sources.

Standard printing paper weights and finishes can appear to be confusing to the uninitiated, but they can also be simplified into a few categories. These papers are the real workhorses of the printing industry, as they are readily available and generally perform with consistent results.

The Machiavellian Paper Weight Principle

LET'S GET THE BASICS OUT OF THE WAY. Paper is categorized by *basis weight*, a term that takes on relatively bizarre characteristics in application. Basis weight is the weight of five hundred sheets of a given grade of paper, in that particular grade of paper's standard parent size, which varies from grade to grade. There are explanations galore for this system, most of which only serve to justify its existence while avoiding common sense. The best explanation is that it's a tradition. In a fast-paced world where technology becomes obsolete within a few months and information is flooding us from all directions, it can be amusing to ponder that an 8 ½ x 11- inch sheet of 50-pound offset paper feels just like a sheet of 20-pound bond. What follows are the reasons these issues may be important to you.

Bond

BOND PAPER IS RELATIVELY INEX-PENSIVE and is generally used in cut 8 ½ x 11-inch sizes for letters, copying, and business forms. It sees enormous use in the business environment, and is often used for quick printing and simple letterheads. The parent size sheet of bond paper is 17 x 22 inches. Five hundred sheets of 11 x 17-inch 20-pound bond paper weighs 20 pounds. This paper comes in a reasonably smooth finish and a variety of often-garish colors. It is perfectly adequate for the purposes it's designed to fulfill.

Writing Paper

WRITING PAPER IS A HIGH-GRADE BOND PAPER, often made with a percentage of cotton and used for stationery packages designed to convey a luxurious image. It comes in a variety of finishes and colors. Finishes can be smooth, laid, eggshell, or linen. The colors generally range from bright white to a variety of neutral hues. This is the paper for classy image packages, and is generally available with matching envelopes and cover weights for business cards. The parent size of writing paper is the same as bond; 17 x 22 inches. Five hundred sheets of 24-pound writing paper this size 24 pounds. Writing papers are often watermarked, which can be an important element in conveying an upper-crust image. Maintaining the correct orientation of the watermark on finished letterheads is always a major concern for printers.

106
...

**GRAPHIC
DESIGNER'S
COLOR
HANDBOOK**

The spongy surfaces of uncoated textured paper tend to increase dot gain and line size. Whether laid, linen, or felt finished, they require increased printing pressure to impress the ink image into the *valleys* of the finish, which ultimately adds to the gain. Fine line screens with sharp detail are better reproduced on smooth coated stock.

The Parent Size Conundrum

A SIGNIFICANT AND OFTEN DETRIMENTAL ELEMENT of writing papers is the combination of *parent* size and watermark. Although the basic parent size is 11 x 17 inches, these papers are also available in larger sheet sizes, 22 $\frac{1}{2}$ x 34 inches and sometimes up to 23 x 35 inches. These sizes often create limitations in the image area that can be printed, particularly if the paper is watermarked and the design calls for bleeds. All sheetfed printing presses require a *gripper* allowance for mechanical pincers to hold the sheets. The gripper is generally $\frac{3}{8}$ inch and represents a "no print" zone on the leading edge of each sheet. Images that bleed also generally require an oversized press sheet to allow for trimming.

Printers will try to squeeze as much image area as possible onto any given press sheet, but the end result is sometimes a slightly undertrimmed letterhead. The answer is to print letterheads that have bleed designs on a larger parent size, which results in a good deal of wasted paper and higher costs for long runs. When writing papers are available in 23 x 35-inch parent sheets, the sheet can be cut into thirds for the press, and the letterheads can be printed *two-up* on the press sheets. This solution offers tremendous savings in paper costs, and usually maintains the watermark in a *right-reading* orientation.

For the best results in envelope printing, print on 'flat' sheets and then have the sheets converted into finished envelopes. This will ensure consistency across the print run.

Many image packages (envelopes, letterhead, and business cards) are designed so that the envelopes print in four colors or with bleeds. This can present one of a printer's most interesting challenges. Depending on the nature of the bleed, many printers can get away with printing premanufactured envelopes on small presses. Envelopes present an inherently unstable printing surface because of the uneven multiple layers and slight variations in their manufacture. This can create a difficult proposition for the press operator, and the results are sometimes less than desirable.

For critical jobs with bleeds, and for virtually all four-color jobs with high expectations, the practical approach is to have your print rep quote the job to print on flat sheets and then have the sheets converted into finished envelopes. Printers experienced with this process will probably include prediecutting the printed sheets on a letterpress before sending them to the envelope converter. This helps ensure accuracy and first-class results. Without the diecutting, most converters will not guarantee a conversion accuracy of less than $\frac{1}{8}$ inch. This can be a tricky area for graphic designers striving to quote accurately for clients, and often leads to discord that can travel from the client to the designer, to the printer, to the envelope converter, and then right back up the ladder. It's always best to know your printer's capabilities and to ask for samples and assurances.

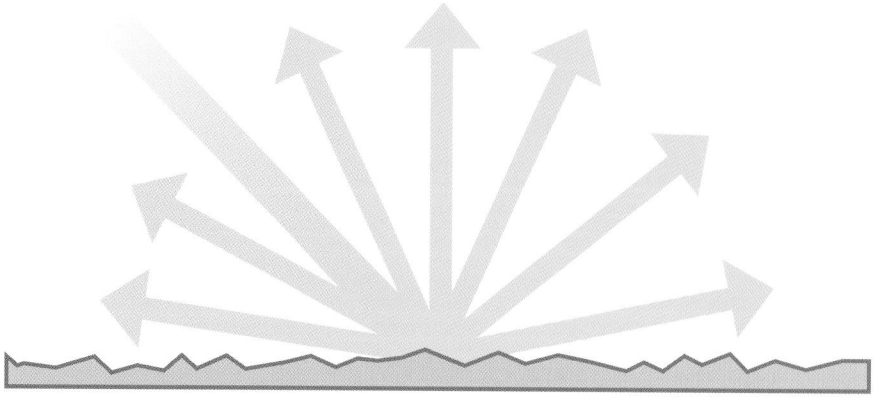

108
...

GRAPHIC
DESIGNER'S
COLOR
HANDBOOK

The surface of uncoated papers, as seen in this exploded side view of a single sheet, is rough and uneven. Ambient light in the viewing environment is absorbed and reflected from these surfaces and scattered in many directions, resulting in the dull appearance of ink on these types of paper.

Printing on Writing Paper Surfaces

WRITING PAPER IS GENERALLY VERY WELL MADE under strict quality controls and provides a stable printing surface. For four-color designs, or designs that have a great deal of definition, it's best to choose smooth surfaces. One drawback is that the increased printing pressure required for these papers can cause slight distortions as the press sheets travel through successive printing units. This can lead to misregistration, and the printed images can shift from sheet to sheet as the job is being printed. Linen finishes tend to offer a less spongy surface than laid finishes because the process that produces the cross-hatched linen look also produces a smoother surface.

Laid

Linen

Laid finishes, as illustrated on the top, tend to be spongy, and excaserbate dot gain. The linen finish on the bottom has a pattern that is reminiscent of a weaved linen cloth material. The application of this finish is stamped by hard rollers during the paper making process and produces a hard uncoated printing surface, which will print finer detail in comparison with the laid finish.

Color
in Print

The surfaces of highly calendared uncoated, matte, and dull-coated papers are much smoother than standard uncoated paper and diffuse light in a less exaggerated fashion. The result is more vibrancy in printed images.

Color and Appearance on Writing Paper

WHEN CHOOSING SPECIALLY MIXED colors for writing papers, bear in mind that these papers are uncoated, so you should choose colors using the uncoated pages in the color guidebook. Writing papers are usually available in a variety of relatively neutral colors. The choice of color stock will also affect the ink colors you choose. For critical color matching, it's always a good idea to ask your printer for an ink *drawdown* on a sheet of the job stock. Many ink companies will do this as a service for the printing companies they work with. Some printing companies have the personnel and equipment to provide the service for you directly, though there may be nominal fees for these samples. If you have an established relationship with a printer, you can often receive this service at no charge, particularly if the printer knows that they will be producing the job for you. You'd be surprised at the little extras your print reps will try to provide for you, assuming you offer some reasonable incentive.

Quality coated papers present a smooth surface with great reflective qualities. The combination of clay coatings that hold ink pigments on the surface, and more direct reflection of the viewing light, results in images that shine.

Text Papers

TEXT PAPERS ARE AVAILABLE in an array of textures and colors. Some are manufactured in finishes and colors identical to those in writing paper lines, and are excellent choices as companion brochures for stationery image packages. The basic parent size of text paper is 25 x 38 inches. Text paper is available in 60, 70, and 80 pound weights, and in cover weights of 65, 80, and 110 pounds. All are appropriate for booklet covers and business cards.

Offset and Book Papers

THESE PAPERS ARE SIMILAR IN APPEARANCE and print characteristics. The basic parent size of book paper is 25 x 38 inches, which is ideal for book production because it provides ample image and trimming area. Surfaces range from vellum to smooth finishes.

These papers are uncoated and subject to dot gain, which makes ultra high-resolution images difficult to reproduce. The maximum line screen effectively used on these uncoated papers is 150, with 133 generally being the most acceptable choice.

The quality and price of offset and book papers covers a tremendous range. The lower end of the spectrum will provide adequate results for spot-color and black-and-white projects. Solids and screens tend to have a mottled appearance, halftones are subject to plugging, and *show through* is common. Papers at the high end of the scale are very opaque with good ink holdout. These are often highly *calendared*, a process through which the paper is passed through a series of calendaring, or polishing, rollers in the finishing stages.

112
...

GRAPHIC
DESIGNER'S
COLOR
HANDBOOK

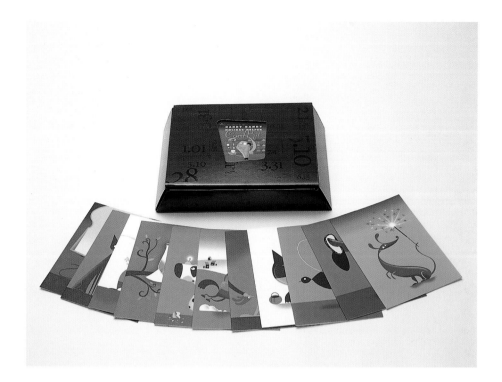

On the high end of the book paper scale, you can achieve absolutely beautiful printing results. These papers, sometimes referred to as *opaque*, have extremely smooth printing surfaces, hold solid images nicely, and handle halftones and screens very well. (Courtesy Paul Baker Printing, CMB Design, and Image Wise Packaging.)

Printing on Uncoated Paper

PRINTING AND HANDLING CHARAC-TERISTICS of uncoated papers on sheetfed presses are significantly different than those of coated papers. They require more time to dry, because more ink is required in comparison to coated paper, and the inks don't set as quickly due to the spongy nature of the sheet surfaces. As a result, turning uncoated sheets too quickly to print the other side can result in ink *picking off* onto the *impression cylinders* of the press. The printing image is transferred to the paper as the latter passes between the blanket cylinder that carries the image and the *impression cylinders*, which apply tremendous pressure. A build up of excess ink on any of these cylinders will create serious problems and force the pressman to halt the job for maintenance or additional drying time.

Coated Paper

AS A RULE, COATED PAPER IS THE BEST CHOICE for high-quality reproduction of heavy color and fine detail. Coated paper offers a smooth, ink-receptive surface and usually has excellent printing and handling characteristics.

Coated paper quickly absorbs the vehicle of ink, leaving the pigment on the surface. Because of this, coated papers require a much thinner ink application than do uncoated papers to achieve an even stronger density. Ink printed on coated paper can feel dry to the touch within a few minutes, and jobs can often be handled within a few hours of coming off the press. The ink vehicle may still be far from dry, but being absorbed into the fibers of the paper underneath the coating, this fluidity doesn't present a problem as long as the surface is dry enough to handle.

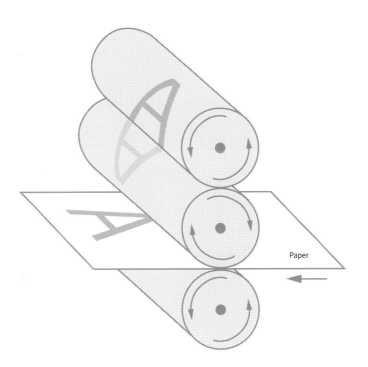

Paper

In this simplified illustration of offset printing, the top cylinder carries the printing plate and the middle blanket cylinder transfers the image to the paper. The impression cylinder is on the bottom. The relationship among these cylinders is critical, and settings are measured in thousandths of an inch. Buildup of ink residue from previously printed jobs, or from the backside of the current job, can create maintenance problems.

Multicolor sheetfed presses have devices that deposit a thin layer of vegetable-based powder across the surface of each sheet as it leaves the final printing unit to be deposited in a stack (usually referred to as the *pile*). The powder helps keep the sheets separated for the few moments required for the ink to begin setting. This powder is absorbed into the ink as it dries, and is seldom—if ever—noticed by the end user. Failure of the powdering device can cause the paper to stick together, which can ruin the job. Rigorous maintenance of these devices is a high priority for every press operator.

If the press applies more ink to the sheet than can be absorbed, the ink transfers to the next available location, which is usually the next sheet deposited in the delivery pile.

The result is called *setting-off*. Set-off can be caused by failure of the powdering device, or overinking, and is a common reason for spoilage and reprints.

Commercial web presses aren't subject to the same problems when using coated papers. On these machines, the job is printed on both sides as the continuous web of paper travels through the printing units, and through a superheated tunnel. This is followed by a series of *chill rollers* that cool the paper, set the ink, and send the web to the folding or cutting attachment at the delivery, or end, of the press.

114
...

GRAPHIC
DESIGNER'S
COLOR
HANDBOOK

Here, the press operator compares a press sheet to the approved proof during the run. The highly reflective quality of gloss-coated paper is apparent. (Courtesy Heidelberg USA, Inc.)

Grades and Color Appearance on Coated Papers

ACCURATE COLOR REPRODUCTION is best achieved on coated stocks. The clay coating absorbs ink rapidly, leaving the color pigments and hardening agents on the surface with far greater fidelity than is possible with uncoated paper.

Grades of coated papers vary primarily in the amount of clay applied to the surfaces and the degree of polishing, or *buffing*, performed on the surface. Common grades of coated paper are three, two, one, premium, and cast coated. The three grades have the least amount of clay. Premium paper has a much higher clay content, with more buffing, to achieve a very smooth and consistent finish. Costs vary tremendously from lower to higher grades because of the manufacturing time and extra steps taken to achieve premium finishes.

Varnishes and Aqueous Coating— A Cheap Thrill

ADDING VARNISHES CAN ENHANCE and protect printed images. This is often a good idea when printing heavy color coverage on dull and matte coated stocks, as it offers protection from scratching and scuffing. Applying gloss varnish over four-color work printed on dull coated papers can make images pop. Dull varnishes are more subdued, and when used on gloss-coated paper can provide a great deal of contrast against the shiny surface of the paper. Depending on your printer, the cost of adding varnishes can be minimal, and it can pay to do some comparison shopping.

Flood and Spot Varnishing

PRESS OPERATORS CAN APPLY VARNISH to press sheets in two ways. *Flood varnishing* applies a coat of varnish over the entire sheet. Many printers do this allowing a heavy flow of varnish onto the inking rollers, which transfers to a blank plate, then onto the blanket and the paper as it passes through the press.

Spot varnishing requires the use of a plate exposed with the images to be varnished, in exactly the same fashion that ink is applied. As with inked images, the varnish images can be relatively complex to produce.

Printed images on uncoated paper have a much duller appearance than on coated paper because the spongy surface absorbs and scatters reflected light. Some printers have tried in vain to apply varnish to uncoated paper in an effort to achieve a glossy effect. While this is possible on highly calendared smooth finishes, the result is often so mottled that the idea is quickly scrapped. If you need a glossy appearance on uncoated stock, the best solution is a UV coating, which requires specialized equipment and involves an application of thick polymer coating that dries almost instantly under intense UV lamps. There are additional costs for the UV coating process, but this step provides a smooth and highly reflective surface.

Varnishing . . . Who Needs It?

ON SOME PRESSES, VARNISHING may require additional passes and add considerably to the job's cost. Many print shops with five- and six-color presses will bid the cost of four-color work competitively against other four-color presses. In these cases, the addition of a varnishing plate increases the cost of the job only by the plates and varnishes used. Many multithousand dollar printing jobs can be varnished for only a few hundred dollars more than the bid price.

Depending on the nature of your project and the paper stock it's to be printed on, your print rep may strongly encourage the addition of varnish for protecting the paper's finish. Printers sometimes add varnish at no cost to protect the interests of a reluctant client who doesn't think the job would be ruined in the binding and finishing processes. If your print rep insists, get another opinion from another rep. If they both insist, it would be wise to pay heed.

Aqueous Coating

MANY MULTICOLOR PRINTING PRESSES are manufactured with in-line aqueous coating units. These units apply coating in the same fashion as flood varnishing, with a layer of aqueous coating covering the entire sheet. Some manufacturers have developed systems for applying spot aqueous coatings with specially manufactured blankets that transfer coating to the paper in specific areas.

As the name implies, aqueous coating is a water-based material and is manufactured in finishes ranging from dull to high gloss. Drying systems on these presses are incredibly efficient, and these coatings can feel dry to the touch within moments.

The five gray towers on this press are the printing units. The lower gray tower is the aqueous coating unit. (Courtesy Heidelberg USA, Inc.).

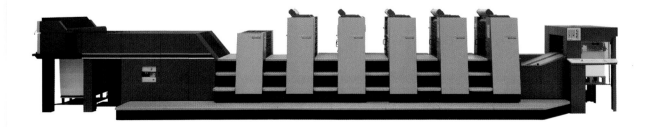

SUMMARY

Color
in Print

PAPER CHOICES HAVE A HUGE IMPACT on the overall effect of your designs and can be instrumental in your client's reactions to the projects you design for them. Learning the printing characteristics of paper will enable you and your clients to make choices that will provide reliable results. You can also help your clientele make the most cost effective paper choices by understanding the variables of paper availability. This can help define your options, prevent last-minute disappointments, and goes a long way toward establishing that you have their best interests in mind. Ultimately, this knowledge helps build a foundation for enduring relationships.

WORKING WITH YOUR PRINTER

IF YOU'RE A PRINTER, IT'S IMPORTANT to establish a strong working relationship with the graphic design community. If you're a designer, it's equally important to keep this relationship open and harmonious. A mutual alliance can make a world of difference not only to your clients but also to your design career. For most print professionals, there's no such thing as a dumb question, and when it comes to color, there are plenty of questions to be asked. Specialists involved in printing can be terrific sources of information. The more you learn, the more quickly you'll realize that printers are always impressed by designers who know their stuff.

This chapter serves as a designer's introduction to selecting and working with a printer. It describes typical print facilities, the services and technologies available, guidelines for color press checks, and how to avoid nightmare scenarios. Working with color, from design to print, can be intimidating, especially when it comes time to do proofs and press checks. All successful color designers have learned from their printer and have a savvy understanding of the evolution of their color projects.

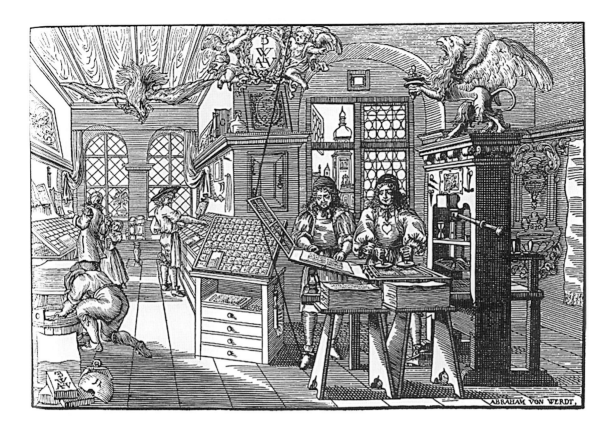

Choosing Your Printer Wisely

HOW DO YOU SELECT A RELIABLE printer for your color work? Many medium-to-large printers don't feel a need to invest in splashy advertising in the telephone directory because they don't rely on walk-in or call-in business. One of the best ways to find out about printers is to call other experienced graphic designers and ask whom they are using. Don't be afraid to also ask whom they're *not* using. With several telephone calls, you'll probably notice a pattern of printers who get a lot of repeat business and probably a few who don't. Once you've developed a list of potential printers, a few phone calls will probably result in a minor stampede of print sales reps. One benefit of new print technologies is that they are rapidly closing gaps in the quality of work that printers are capable of producing, and competition for your business is increasing at the same pace.

Printing Sales Reps

MOST MEDIUM-SIZE PRINTING companies, and virtually all of the large ones, maintain a staff of full-time *print reps*. The technical knowledge and experience of sales reps ranges from those who have degrees in graphic arts, to those who have spent years in the trade as press operators and prepress technicians to those who were selling shoes last week. Good sales reps have one thing in common: If they don't know the answers to your questions off the tops of their heads, they'll get answers for you—and quickly. Modern print production is complicated and rapidly changing, and while it may be unrealistic to expect someone to have a practical answer to every query, it's not unrealistic to expect a timely response.

Working with Your Print Rep

THE RELATIONSHIP BETWEEN designer and print rep begins with clear communication. At the root of this association is establishing responsibility and rapport. From day one, it's important that you and your print rep scrutinize the project and discuss all aspects regarding color, specifications, and submissions. The time to deal with problems involving color is at the beginning, because a concern that isn't brought up before production begins can lead to major charges in a hurry. Color is an expensive endeavor and changes can be costly.

Questions to ask a potential printer and/or print rep:

1. Do you offer tours of your printing facility?

2. Are you amenable to press checks?

3. Can I have contact with your prepress department?

4. How is your financing handled?

5. What proofing systems do you use?

6. What types of presses do you run?

7. How much, if any, of your work do you contract out?

8. If you do farm out work, do you notify your clients beforehand?

9. Can you provide imposition dummies that fit your formats for multiple-page projects?

10. Have you printed jobs identical to, or similar to, mine?

11. Can you provide samples and proofs of those projects?

12. How do you handle change orders and extra charges?

13. How do you handle paper problems that cause printing deficiencies?

14. What are your policies for reprinting jobs that are unacceptable to me?

15. Do you keep to your deadlines?

16. How do you handle shipping and delivery?

17. Do you charge for delivery?

18. What do you expect from a designer?

The key to any successful color project is communication between designer and printer. When discussing a project, such as this two-sided brochure, the designer and print rep should evaluate it carefully to determine that it is an appropriate job for this printing company.

What Is A Wetland?

Before undertaking any activity that may impact a wetland, you should have some understanding of basic wetland principles. Wetlands are considered transition zones between open water and uplands. Wetland types in Montana include sloughs, margins around lakes, ponds and streams, wet meadows, fens, and potholes. Even so, many folks have separate ideas of what constitutes these areas and as a result they have different definitions of wetlands.

Wetland: A Legal Definition

Government agencies have adopted a consistent wetland definition developed jointly by the Army Corps of Engineers (ACOE) and Environmental Protection Agency (EPA), in "The Wetlands Delineation Manual of 1987":

Wetlands are those areas that are inundated or saturated by surface or groundwater at a frequency and duration sufficient to support, and that under normal circumstances do support, a prevalence of vegetation typically adapted for life in saturated soil conditions. Wetlands generally include swamps, marshes, bogs, and similar areas.

This wetland definition is based on hydrology, hydric soils and hydrophytic vegetation. Only areas that meet all three criteria are considered wetlands subject to federal regulation.

Key Federal Laws Affecting Wetlands

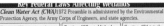

Clean Water Act (CWA)/1972 Preamble is administered by the Environmental Protection Agency, the Army Corps of Engineers, and state agencies.

Section 401 requires that states review and certify permits that may result in pollution discharges into surface waters and wetlands	Section 402 established a permit system required for any discharge of pollutants from a point source into navigable waters	Section 404 jointly administered by the ACOE and EPA, governs dredging and filling of land

National Environmental Policy Act	NEPA requires federal agencies to take action to minimize the destruction, loss or degradation of wetlands and to preserve the natural values of wetlands on federal lands
Executive Order 11990	Requires federal agencies take action to minimize destruction, loss or degradation of wetlands and to preserve natural values of wetlands on federal lands
Rivers and Harbors Act	Gives authority to the ACOE to prohibit discharge of solids or construction into tidal and navigable and adjacent waters
1985 Food Securities Act	"Swampbuster," denies some federal subsidies for conversion of wetlands to agricultural uses
Endangered Species Act	Administered by U.S. Fish and Wildlife Service, protects wetlands that offer unique habitat for endangered and threatened species

State Laws Affecting Wetlands

The Montana Environmental Policy Act and two Montana Administrative Rules regulate activities that may affect wetlands.

Tribal Laws Affecting Wetlands

Tribal governments in Montana safeguard the health, welfare, and economic security of their people. They protect aquatic resources—including wetlands—that are critical for water quality, fisheries and wildlife. The Confederated Salish and Kootenai Tribe and Blackfeet Nation currently have regulations and ordinances in place. Tribes on the other five Montana reservations are also developing wetland programs and strategies. If you own land adjacent to or within reservation boundaries, you need to consult with the appropriate tribal government office about wetlands on your property.

Navigating The Permit Maze

Typical Question	Answer	Permit Name	Agency	Contact	Waiting Period
"I want to build an access road across the wetland to get to my new house. Do I need a permit?"	YES	404	ACOE, or DEQ regarding water quality issues	Allan Steinle, ACOE, 406-441-1375. John Wardell, EPA, 406-441-1140	About 30 days for projects of minimal environmental impact; 60-120 days for major impact.
"I want to clear away some shrubs and brush on my wetland. Can I use a bulldozer and grader?"	Heavy equipment requires a permit. Hand-held equipment (chainsaws, shovels) may be used without permit.	404	ACOE, or DEQ regarding water quality issues	Allan Steinle or staff 406-441-1375	About 30 days.
"I want to build a pond. Do I need a permit?"	Yes. Permits needed for heavy equipment in a wetland or drainage area; also for water rights.	404 / Water Right Permit	ACOE, or DEQ for water quality issues; DNRC Water Rights Bureau	Allan Steinle or staff 406-441-1375 DNRC Staff 406-444-6610	About 30 days.
"I want to build a gravel bar to direct the flow of stream water into the irrigation ditch. Do I need a permit?"	YES	310	Submit application for 310 permit to local CD. Depending on nature of work and the location, DEQ and DNRC may need to be contacted.	Local County Conservation District (CD)	Local CD (meets monthly) determines if permit needed, and will schedule inspection and submit a report at next meeting. A 310 permit is valid for a year. March is a good time to submit application for permit, usually needed by August.
"Do I have a wetland? I need to know for a building project."	Ask NRCS specialist or wetland consultant. If your land contains hydric soil, NRCS will refer you to a wetlands specialist for a wetland delineation. If dredge or fill is needed, ACOE must be consulted.	Swampbuster & possibly 404. If minor disruption (<3 acres), you might proceed under nationwide permit. You need letter from ACOE to confirm.	NRCS, ACOE	Local NRCS (Also provides a technical guide of regional wetland plants.) Allan Steinle or staff 406-441-1375	Time to check soil map (1 hr. to 2 days). Schedule depends on consultant, demands, area of land and coordination with others. Usually 30 days for projects of minimal environmental impact and 60-120 days for major impact.

* For further reference see: "A Guide To Stream Permitting in Montana", March 1997, available from your local conservation district office.

Why Are Wetlands Important?

For decades, we were unaware of the critical functions wetlands perform. In this new century, we understand the importance of keeping natural wetland systems healthy. Montana's remaining wetlands are essential to waterfowl, shorebirds, and other wildlife, water quality, and for providing flood control.

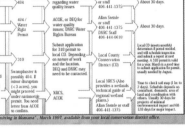

What About Artificial Wetlands?

The Natural Resources Conservation Service (NRCS) defines an artificial wetland as land that was not a wetland under natural conditions, but now exhibits wetland characteristics due to human activities. Human-induced wetlands, like those under irrigation, may meet the requirements of wetlands by water, soils, and vegetation.

It is possible that artificial wetlands may not be subject to provisions of the NRCS Swampbuster Program, but be regulated by the ACOE under Section 404 of the Clean Water Act. The ACOE decides, on a case by case basis, if a human-induced wetland is subject to protection.

Wetlands And Water Rights

Although you may desire an artificial wetland, will you have a water right for the water in that wetland? Unless you have a valid water right, your use of water for that wetland may not be protected against others who desire the use of that water. A water right gives you a property right (and a priority date) that is valid in state Water Court. The Montana Department of Natural Resources and Conservation (DNRC) has

jurisdiction over the issuance of new water use permits, as well as changes of existing water rights to new uses. To find out more about water rights, and whether you have, or can obtain, a water right for an artificial wetland, contact your nearest DNRC Regional Office.

For More Information

Or to request additional materials on wetlands and wetland-related programs available in the state, contact the Montana Watercourse at 406-994-6671.

You may reproduce or copy any portion of this brochure by notifying the Montana Watercourse at the above number. Please acknowledge this publication as the source.

printed on recycled paper

Produced By

Montana Watercourse
P.O. Box 170575
Montana State University
Bozeman, MT 59717
406-994-6671
Funding was provided by the Environmental Protection Agency, Wetlands Grant Program of the Montana Dept. of Environmental Quality.

Copyright. All rights reserved. Printed in the United States of America, August 2000.
Design by Media Works, Bozeman, MT

WETLAND LAWS, PERMITS AND REGULATIONS

Navigating The Maze

Often seen as wastelands, an estimated 25% of Montana's wetlands have vanished in the last century and a half. We now realize that wetlands are critical natural resources.

As our appreciation of wetland functions and values has increased, so has society's commitment to protecting them. Our laws express that commitment, and government regulations help us to implement the laws. This brochure describes wetland protection laws and provides a chart to help you find your way through the sometimes-complicated wetland permitting process. By working together, perhaps we can build a legacy of wetland gains to correct our historic losses.

Wetlands Losses (1780 - 1980)

Data from: Dahl, T.E. 1990. Wetlands Losses in the United States, 1780's to 1980's. US Dept. of Interior, Fish & Wildlife Service, Washington D.C.

122
...

GRAPHIC
DESIGNER'S
COLOR
HANDBOOK

Alaska is famous for the rugged beauty of its mountains, rivers, and coastlines, as well as for the distinctive arts and crafts produced by Alaskan Native artisans. If you are considering purchasing a Native-made art or craft item, it's smart to invest a little time learning about the processes and materials Alaskan Natives use to make these unique and beautiful objects.

Identifying Arts and Crafts Made by Alaskan Natives

Any item produced after 1935 that is marketed with terms like *"Indian," "Native American"* or *"Alaska Native"* must have been made by a member of a state or federally-recognized tribe or a certified Indian artisan. That's the law.

A certified Indian artisan is an individual certified by the governing body of the tribe of their descent as a non-member Indian artisan. For example, it would violate the law to advertise products as *"Inupiaq Carvings"* if the products were produced by someone who isn't a member of the Inupiaq tribe or certified by the tribal governing body as a non-member Alaskan Native artisan of the Inupiaq people.

Qualifiers like *"ancestry," "descent"* and *"heritage"* – used in connection with the terms *"Indian,"* or *"Alaskan Native"* or the name of a particular Indian tribe – don't mean that the craftsperson is a member of an Indian tribe or certified by a tribe. For example, *"Native American heritage"* or *"Yupik descent"* would mean that the artisan is of descent, heritage or ancestry of the tribe. These terms may be used only if they are truthful.

Buying Tips

Alaskan Native arts and crafts are sold through many outlets, including tourist stores, gift shops, art galleries, museums, culture centers, and the Internet. Here are some tips to help you shop wisely:

- Get written proof of any claims the seller makes for the authenticity of the art or craft item you're purchasing.

- Ask if your item comes with a certification tag. Not all authentic Alaskan Native arts and crafts items carry a tag. Those that do may display a **Silver Hand** symbol. This label features a silver hand and the words, *"Authentic Native Handicraft from Alaska."* The **Made in Alaska** emblem is another symbol you may find on some Alaskan-made products. This emblem certifies that the article *"was made in Alaska,"* though not necessarily by an Alaskan Native.

- Get a receipt that includes all the vital information about the value of your purchase, including any oral representations. For example, if a salesperson tells you that the basket you're buying is made of baleen and ivory and was handmade by an Inupiaq artisan, insist that the information is on your receipt.

It can be difficult to distinguish arts and crafts produced by Alaskan Natives from items that are imitations: Price, materials and appearance are important clues to provenance.

- **Price** – The price of a genuine Alaskan Native art or craft item should reflect the quality of craftsmanship, the harmony of the design and the background of the artisan. Genuine pieces produced by skilled Alaskan Native artisans can be expensive.

- **Type of materials** – Materials often used by Alaskan Native artisans include walrus ivory, soapstone, argillite, bone, alabaster, animal furs and skin, baleen and other marine mammal materials.

- **Appearance** – Try to pick up and examine a piece before purchasing it. Some items that appear to be soapstone carvings actually may be made of resin. Real stone is cool to the touch; plastic is warm. Stone also tends to be

heavier than plastic. And a figure that is presented as hand-carved probably isn't if you see or can order 10 more like it that are perfectly uniform or lack surface variations.

Alaskan Native Carvings

Sculptures and carvings by Alaskan Natives vary in size, and usually portray animals or Alaskan people. Before you buy a carved figure, learn about the different mediums that are commonly used. It can help you spot a fake.

Walrus Ivory is one of the more popular and expensive mediums used in Alaskan sculptures. In carvings, *new ivory* often has "breathing cracks," or thin black lines that occur naturally and should add to the beauty of the piece. These lines are caused by abrupt changes in temperatures that the walrus experiences when moving from warm rock "haul-outs" to the icy waters of the Arctic region. By law, new walrus ivory may be carved only by an Alaskan Native and it may be sold only after it has been carved. *Old ivory* can be carved by non-Natives. *Fossil ivory* also may be used, though it is both more rare and more expensive. Because of the differences in the fossilized ivory, no two carvings have the same design or color.

Soapstone is a soft rock with a soapy feel. It's popular with Alaskan Native artists because it's widely available and easy to carve. Soapstone ranges in color from gray to green, and while it scratches easily, it also resists acids, chemicals and heat.

Argillite is a compact rock used primarily by the Haida people of Alaska. It usually has a grayish-brown color and is smooth to the touch.

Bone, usually from whales and other marine animals, is used to create carvings and masks. Bone masks are made from the vertebrae or disk of the Bowhead whale. The color of bone masks ranges from light tan to dark brown. Bone carvings also are used as a way to express the Alaskan Native "way of life." Bone items resemble ivory, but are less expensive.

Alabaster, often a white or translucent stone, also is used as a sculpture medium by Alaskan Natives. Alabaster used in Alaska is imported.

Beyond Carvings

Alaskan Native artisans also produce baskets, dolls, drums, masks, prints, and etchings.

Baleen, also called whalebone, is a flexible material from the jaw of baleen whales. It is used to weave baskets and make etchings. Alaskan Native etchings often portray stories from the artist's unique culture; they're done in a style similar to the scrimshaw technique Boston whalers used in the 1800's.

Alaskan dolls are handcrafted by many Alaskan Native women and reflect unique styles. Dolls often portray the activities of the artist's people. Typically, a doll's clothes and body are made from calf skin (calf skin has taken the place of caribou/reindeer hide materials and is not native to the area), mink, badger, sea otter, arctic rabbit, seal, or beaver. In many dolls, dried marine mammal intestine (which sometimes is bleached naturally in cold temperatures and sun so that it is very white, or has a slight yellowed wax paper look to it) is used for clothing. The hair often is made from musk oxen, and some artists use baleen or ivory for the eyes.

Alaskan Native prints are produced using a variety of techniques. **Serigraphy,** also called **screen printing** or **silk screening,** involves printing through a surface, similar to a stencil technique. **Relief print making** is done from a raised surface, like a cut stone or wood block; **intaglio print making** is created using the recessed image from the surface of etchings or engravings on metal plates of copper and tin. **Lithography** involves the artist using a grease-water technique to apply a variety of colors to the etched design on stone or metal plates.

For More Information

To learn more about Alaskan Native arts and crafts, contact:

Alaska State Council on the Arts
411 West 4th Avenue, Suite 1E
Anchorage, AK 99501-2343
907-269-6610; fax: 907-269-6601
Toll-free: 1-888-278-7424
www.aksca.org

Where to Complain

The FTC works for the consumer to prevent fraudulent, deceptive and unfair business practices in the marketplace and to provide information to help consumers spot, stop and avoid them. To file a complaint or to get free information on consumer issues, call toll-free, 1-877-FTC-HELP (1-877-382-4357), or use the complaint form at www.ftc.gov. The FTC enters Internet, telemarketing, identity theft and other fraud-related complaints into Consumer Sentinel, a secure, online database available to hundreds of civil and criminal law enforcement agencies in the U.S. and abroad.

The **Indian Arts and Crafts Board** refers valid complaints about violations of the Indian Arts and Crafts Act of 1990 to the FBI for investigation and to the Department of Justice for legal action. To file a complaint under the Act, or to get free information about the Act, contact the Indian Arts and Crafts Board, U.S. Department of the Interior, 1849 C Street, N.W., MS 4004-MIB, Washington, D.C. 20240; 202-208-3773; www.iacb.doi.gov.

Complaints to the IACB must be in writing and include the following information:

- The name, address and telephone number of the seller.
- A description of the art or craft item.
- How the item was offered for sale.
- What representations were made about the item, including any claims that the item was made by a member of a particular tribe or statements about its authenticity.
- Any other documentation, such as advertisements, catalogs, business cards, photos, or brochures. Include copies (NOT originals) of documents that support your position.

The **Alaska Attorney General's Office** investigates unfair and deceptive marketing and sales practices in Alaska. To obtain a complaint form, contact the Office of the Attorney General, Consumer Protection Unit, 1031 West 4th Avenue, Suite 200, Anchorage, AK 99501; 907-269-5100; or use the complaint form at www.law.state.ak.us/consumer/index.html.

The Alaska State Council on the Arts, the Federal Trade Commission, the U.S. Department of Interior's Indian Arts and Crafts Board, and the Alaska Attorney General's Office have prepared this brochure to help enhance your appreciation for Alaskan Native arts and crafts.

March 2002

Alaskan Native Art

Your print rep should be able to provide you with samples of work that are comparable to the projects you produce. If you're producing a brochure, you'll want representative samples like these. Bear in mind that print reps will probably only show you samples of their best work.

There to Help You

Print reps are there to help you—not avoid you. If you find that your rep is unresponsive, or doesn't answer your questions to your satisfaction, you should never be afraid to ask for a new one.

As with most professions, communication between buyers and vendors translates to time and money. The printing and design business is no different, especially considering the symbiotic relationship shared between the two fields. The best approach is an open and honest one, where all parties involved—client, designer, and print rep—are free to voice questions, concerns, financial arrangements, and everything in between. The printing process is both complex and specific, and the communication should cover all aspects of a project before, during, and after its completion. Addressing all issues up front—from design to financing, printing, and delivery—is vital, as it can help alleviate potential disasters down the line.

Samples

IF YOU'RE WORKING WITH a new printer, it's important and appropriate to ask for samples and proofs of those samples that are similar to the work that you're doing. Most print reps carry a collection of work that they've done, but those samples may not be appropriate to the nature of your project. Print reps are accustomed to clients requesting samples and there's no shame in asking. If they're resistant, you'd better look for a new printer.

124
...

GRAPHIC
DESIGNER'S
COLOR
HANDBOOK

It's not unreasonable to ask for a few samples along with the proofs that were used to print them. While the printer will certainly want proofs returned to their files, you should be able to inspect them, either in your office or during a tour of the plant.

Industry Standards

Always insist that any change orders be faxed directly to you and that you sign off on them before the printer takes any action. This may not prevent holdups should problems arise, but demonstrating that you understand the concept will serve notice that you're not easily duped. Good printers can rightfully expect you to pay for lost time and material, but they don't try to make a profit from your mistakes.

THE PRINTING INDUSTRY HAS traditionally been entrepreneurial, competitive, and resistant to standardization. The term *industry standards* gets tossed around and misused in numerous ways. You may hear that industry standards allow for 10 to 15 percent additional charges for overruns, that 10 percent shortages are acceptable, or that color variations of impossibly vague degrees are normal. Most printing companies are independently owned, and many regard the concept of industry standardization largely as a means to a competitive edge, rather than making any genuine effort to standardize. In the real world, you and your printer are the ones who set acceptable standards.

Accountability and Responsibility

IT'S NO SECRET THAT PRINTERS, because they're last in line to produce a project, occasionally get blamed when problems occur. The nature of the problem is the key to determining who is ultimately responsible. Although printing errors do happen, it's not always the printer's fault. Errors can slip past the proofing stage, specially ordered paper may get sidetracked in transit, outsource vendors may botch up their end of the job, or the low-rate ground delivery service may lose the shipment. Making assumptions about responsibility can be a mistake if problems arise, and the best way to avoid finger-pointing is to communicate all of your concerns.

Change Orders

IT'S NEVER TOO SOON to discuss *change orders* and their ramifications with your print rep. Some printers will intentionally lowball a printing bid with the expectation of making money on change orders, charging the client for every extra step they take in the production process. Be specific about your concerns, and get specific answers. For example, a client may think the printer is responsible for delivery to multiple local destinations, but this usually isn't the case. And if there's a relatively simple error in one color on a single image, some printers will insist on charging hefty fees for reproofing the entire job. You can ask for a simple spot proof of the correction, but make sure the printer's policy allows for it.

Change Order

Client:				Job No:		
Project:						

Date:	AA/HE:	By(Init.)	Description	Amount of Time Spent:	Date:	By(Init.)	Price:

Faxed to Client:	Date:	Time:	Original Price:
Faxed By:			Total Additional Charges Itemized:
CLIENT SIGNATURE:			**TOTAL AS OF THIS C.O. FORM:**
(Please Sign and Fax back as soon as possible)			

126
...

GRAPHIC
DESIGNER'S
COLOR
HANDBOOK

Prepress and Proofing Sources and Standards

MOST PRINTERS TRY HARD to project the image that they produce superior work, and this is often evident in their presentation of proofs and the types of proofing systems they use. Printers are generally committed to one brand or type of proofing system, particularly with the onset of direct-to-plate technology. The capital outlay for proofing systems is significant when coupled with the hardware required for outputting plates with the same systems. The benefit to the print buyer is that printers generally make every effort to establish that the systems they use produce good color results.

Service Bureaus and Color Houses

A NUMBER OF SMALL TO MEDIUM-sized printing companies still rely on *service bureaus* to handle their scanning and prepress production. These prepress houses serve a wide variety of clients with the variable of not knowing the final application or limitations of the printing equipment. Most prepress houses use working parameters and ranges for acceptable results in the finished product. This is one reason why it's important to ask for samples of printed material *and* proofs of samples. Because of press variables outside the service bureau's control, it's possible to generate a proof that can't reasonably be reproduced by the equipment on which the job will be printed. As the designer, you deserve to know the source of your proofs, with assurances that they can be reasonably duplicated on press.

Service Bureaus and the Future

MOST PRINTING COMPANIES strive to develop consistent protocols resulting in final proofs that can be reasonably matched on the shop's printing equipment. This is a key element of customer confidence and business survival for multicolor printers. It's also one of many reasons that traditional prepress houses are falling on hard times.

In years past, prepress houses provided a valuable service to designers and printing companies. Scanning devices were frightfully expensive and required full-time production to justify the cost, which was well beyond the scope of most medium-sized printers. With well over half of all commercial printing companies considered medium sized, this presented a huge market. Economically, it made sense to send electronic files out to specialists for preparation and proofing, while focusing capital investments on printing presses and bindery equipment—a daunting fiscal challenge in itself.

These figures illustrate an example of an excellent proof outsourced by a printer to a service bureau and then reproduced poorly on the printer's ailing press. This is an unfortunate case where the proofing source exceeded the printer's capacity.

Working
with Your
Printer

Prepress houses and service bureaus with a solid clientele are still investing in high-end drum scanning equipment and sophisticated color-management systems. Here, a technician prepares transparencies for scanning. (Courtesy Heidelberg USA, Inc.

A scanner operator makes adjustments using an integrated color-management system. (Courtesy Heidelberg USA, Inc.)

Direct-to-plate technology has also had a huge impact on prepress houses. Virtually all printers who have invested in direct-to-plate systems have also invested in direct proofing systems that accurately reflect the reproduction capabilities of their presses.

Increasingly computer-savvy designers have also taken a bite out of the specialized prepress market. Good software and color-management systems are available, and designers who once outsourced medium-quality scanning to prepress houses can now do so themselves using desktop hardware.

Prepress houses are still operating successfully, and provide valuable services to designers and printers. For designers, a relationship with prepress services can enhance design quality, and allow the designer to finalize color files before choosing printers. This can be particularly advantageous for projects that may go to press some distance from the design agency. For the smaller printers that haven't established in-house output systems, prepress providers are the critical link to working with electronic files.

Service bureaus and prepress houses lie in the path of technology that is forcing reevaluations and new directions. Some have successfully made a transition to direct-to-press color printing, while maintaining more traditional magazine and quality-conscious advertising agency clientele.

Color Scanning:
DO IT YOURSELF OR SEND IT OUT?

THE CAPABILITIES OF TABLETOP and low-profile flatbed scanners have increased dramatically in the past few years, but for the highest-quality four-color scanning, high-end drum scanners still reign thanks to their definition, resolution, and color fidelity. This is due in part to the almost infinite color adjustments permitted by high-end color management systems. For medium-quality color work, you can get good results on many relatively inexpensive tabletop scanners. But high-quality work requires the sophisticated equipment that printers and service bureaus have invested in. By experimenting with in-house scanning equipment and sending the files out for gang proofing, good designers will quickly recognize their in-house limitations, and send out for scans on the appropriate jobs.

Sophisticated tabletop scanners, such as the model shown here, are now within the budgets of many designers. Instead of relying on your imaging service, you can use these products perform much of your scanning in-house. However, if quality expectations are high, you'll still get the best results by farming the work to a service bureau equipped with costly drum scanners. (Courtesy Heidelberg USA, Inc.)

A printing facility's general appearance is a good indicator of how your projects will be treated. The notion that printing is inherently dirty is nonsense. Good printers take pride in the condition of their shops and their equipment. Bad ones don't. (Courtesy Heidelberg USA, Inc.

130
...

GRAPHIC
DESIGNER'S
COLOR
HANDBOOK

Facility Tours

A few printers have one basic rule of quality control: Give me twenty-five good samples for the client, and ship the rest to the mailing house. Bad print jobs are sent out every day, and it behooves you to ensure that yours won't be one of them.

AS A DESIGNER, you should not hesitate to ask your print rep about touring the printing facility. Good printers are usually proud of the shops they keep, and any reluctance to permit visits should raise a big red flag. Some printing conglomerates hire sales reps to work specific geographic areas and send print jobs through hubs to any of several facilities. If your projects don't require press checking and close oversight, these resources may have financial benefits. The major risk is that your only proof of a successfully completed project is the handful of samples your print rep gives you—and you can bet that they were handpicked.

You can learn quite a bit about a printer's capabilities and attention to detail by the condition of the shop. Your print rep may be decked out in a three-piece Armani suit, but warning bells should be sounding if he takes you on a tour of a messy plant. This is also a good opportunity to meet with the sales manager. Establishing a relationship with the manager puts you in a much stronger position should communication problems arise with your rep.

Busy print shops work with thousands of pieces of paper every day, and sooner or later an unruly sheet hits the floor. Whether it stays there or not is the responsibility of the crew and the shop management. Clean walkways, good lighting, and a friendly crew are signs of a well-run operation that will probably have a designer's best interests in mind. (Courtesy Heidelberg USA, Inc.)

On your tour of the plant, note the press carts stacked with freshly printed sheets. Are they neat and orderly as illustrated here? Attention to these details will be reflected in the attention paid to your project. (Courtesy Heidelberg USA, Inc.)

A Well-Adjusted Press

FOR ANY PRINTING PRESS to achieve its maximum color gamut, it must be well maintained, properly adjusted, and operated with the discerning eye of an experienced press operator. Many of the printing industry's technological advances are focused on streamlining the front end. Printing presses themselves have undergone massive changes and improvements, but their essential function is little changed from what they were designed to do years ago: Apply a few micrometers of ink to a whisker-thin piece of paper with as little harm as possible to the original image.

Printing presses represent some of the most enduring machinery that's still used, and equipment manufactured in the 1960s is bought, sold, and operated every day. One of our favorite printers recently upgraded his shop with two acquisitions: A new film-output system, and a two-color 40-inch press manufactured in 1964. Good press reproduction often defies dating, and we've seen several jobs printed on this thirty-nine-year-old machine that easily compare with work done on the most modern equipment.

The essential ingredient in this process is the operator and/or pressroom manager who understands the subtleties of any given press. These nuances often appear in the visual and mechanical information the operator receives with each press sheet pulled and inspected from the delivery pile. Experienced operators know how to read ink densities, interpret color bars, and spot telltale signs of impending trouble, and they can ward off problems before they occur. Many press operators even *listen* for signals, and can tell that all is well by the sound of a smoothly running press.

Digital Imaging

DIGITAL THERMAL- AND LASER-IMAGING equipment has advanced tremendously in speed, quality, and value. Digital imagers can produce bound booklets—with photo-quality, 600-dpi, four-color images; tab inserts; and variable data for personalizing and mailing addresses—directly from electronic files. This technology is feeding the print-on-demand market with exceptional imagery and resolution.

On-demand printing systems, such as Heidelberg's black-and-white Digimaster, can streamline the production process by generating bound booklets directly from electronic files. Going direct to press with these systems lets you produce exactly the number of copies needed, and you can easily make copy changes on subsequent runs. (Courtesy Heidelberg USA, Inc.)

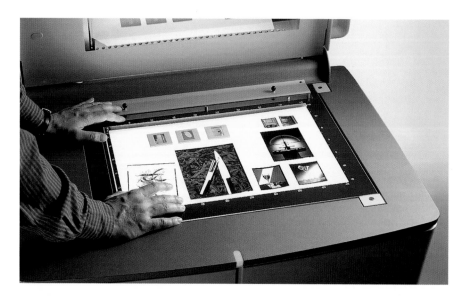

Heidelberg's Nexpress is a more advanced color digital-imaging system that produces bound booklets, with tab inserts, and 600-dpi photo-quality images directly from electronic files. (Courtesy Heidelberg USA, Inc.)

Computer-to-Press Printing

THE CONCEPTS OF computer-to-press (CTP) printing are changing rapidly as technologically advanced equipment comes to market. Virtually all printing done today is digital in some form. Most design work is produced with computer software, jobs can be processed for laser printing, film output, and direct-to-plate or computer-to-press output. With this in mind, it's extremely important for designers to understand the CTP process.

Direct-imaging technology for printing presses is based on the same processes used to image film. From relatively humble beginnings in the late 1980s, to the first commercially available direct-imaging press introduced by Heidelberg in 1991, this technology is filling a huge demand for short-run, good-quality multicolor printing.

Designed for press runs as low as five hundred, this technology allows you to cost-effectively produce four-color work in lower quantities than you can with conventional prepress and printing processes.

In a way, we've come full circle: These presses represent an early form of direct-to-press technology. The presses were prepared with hand-set type and wood blocks, and inked up for a press proof. With the proof okayed, the press was ready to run. In two weeks, this machine could produce the volume of work that would take modern direct-imaging equipment about fifteen minutes. (Courtesy Heidelberg USA, Inc.)

Proofing mechanisms for CTP presses, while not accurate for critical color matching, lets you proof content before initializing the imaging systems. Once the proofs are approved, you can burn images from the electronic file directly to the plate cylinders on press, and print the first sheets for inspection in less than ten minutes. The technology permits these fast setup times in part because images are burned into the plates in nearly perfect registration. Such variables as developing and hanging plates on the press as a separate step have been eliminated.

CTP presses operate in a similar fashion to conventional presses, with a series of printing units applying ink in conventional CMYK sequences. These presses use inks that are comparable in pigment composition to standard offset printing inks, and printed sheets appear similar.

The print quality of these systems can range from medium, at 1,250 dpi, to very good, at 2,400 dpi with 150-line screens, and approaches the quality levels possible on conventional offset presses. Press sizes range from models that can handle 13 x 18 inch sheets, up to a full-size 40-inch press.

As with conventional offset presses, CTP presses have printing units for each of the four process colors. The Heidelberg press illustrated has a compact design, with all four color-printing units configured in a semicircle around a single common impression cylinder. One of the real innovations in this technology is the plate-imaging system, consisting of a spool of silicon-coated printing surfaces that can produce about three dozen separate plates on each unit. These plates are automatically fed and clamped around the printing cylinder, and the printing image is burned onto each through a laser array in a process similar that used by laser recorders that produce film for printing. The silicon layer repels ink and the burned images accept ink, making the process waterless. With the images burned, the press is ready for inking and printing the first set of makeready sheets. Final adjustments are made via computer, and the job is ready to run.

This cutaway side view shows how the four process-color printing units surround a single common-impression cylinder. One benefit of this design is that misregistration is nearly eliminated. (Courtesy Heidelberg USA, Inc.)

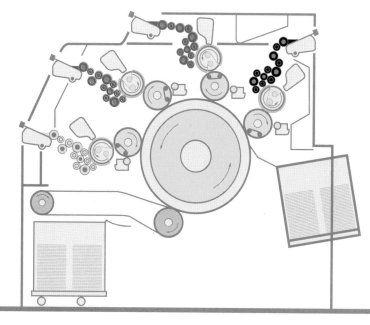

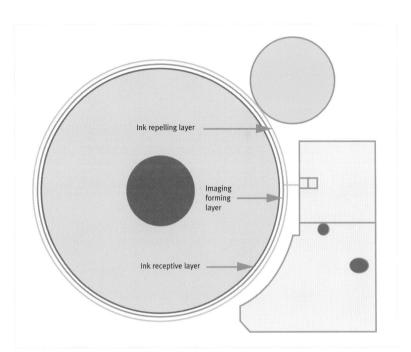

Ink repelling layer

Imaging forming layer

Ink receptive layer

In a computer-to-press system, plates on spools are automatically fed and clamped around a printing cylinder. The image to be printed is burned to the plate directly from digital files. (Courtesy Heidelberg USA, Inc.)

Laser-imaging arrays in a CTP system, as shown in this diagram, are similar to those used in laser recorders that produce film. (Courtesy Heidelberg USA, Inc.)

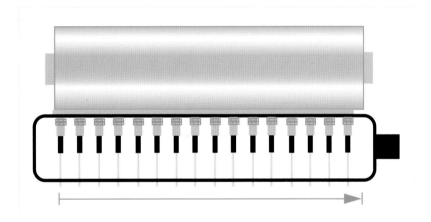

In a CTP system, ink is repelled by the plate's silicon layer, but adheres to the area of the plate burned by the laser. (Courtesy Heidelberg USA, Inc.)

138
...

GRAPHIC
DESIGNER'S
COLOR
HANDBOOK

From one end to the other, computer-to-press systems offer the same features as their big brothers in amazingly compact units. These presses can print affordable, high-quality four-color work, and have opened opportunities for designers in the growing marketplace for short-run, on-demand printing. (Courtesy Heidelberg USA, Inc.)

A CTP system uses CMYK inks similar in pigment composition to standard offset printing inks. Magenta and cyan inking units are shown here. (Courtesy Heidelberg USA, Inc.)

Print on Demand and a Portent of Things to Come

BEFORE THE ADVENT of direct-imaging presses, the costs for printing good-quality four-color work in short runs of five hundred copies or so was often prohibitive. Whether the press run was five hundred or five hundred thousand, the cost of preparing files was exactly the same. For short runs, the cost of file preparation could actually exceed the cost of printing. When producing low-volume projects, print buyers often simplified their designs to one or two colors that could be printed at reasonable costs on small offset duplicators, thus avoiding the additional expenses of preparing four-color files, proofs, and plates.

With computer-to-press imaging, files can be prepared for a short press run to fill a current need, and saved for low-cost reprints if the customer requires additional copies in the future. With conventional processes, uncertainty about the number of copies needed often leads to print overruns. Because the cost of file preparation and press setup has already been incurred, the only costs for overruns are paper, press time, and storage. For projects with guaranteed overrun requirements, this approach makes economic sense. Without guarantees, it can be a costly gamble.

Print on demand, while still in relative infancy, is a growing market, and press manufacturers and printers will likely be moving more in this direction.

Submitting Color Projects to Your Printer

140
...

GRAPHIC
DESIGNER'S
COLOR
HANDBOOK

CLEAR JOB SPECIFICATIONS ARE essential when communicating your expectations to the printer. Some printers prefer that you use their own specification sheets, while others are happy to use yours. Establishing your own checklist is the safest way to ensure that your bases are covered. Your specific needs may vary slightly, but this list describes the minimum specifications you should provide. Once you have mastered this submission process, it will be invaluable to your time and reputation.

Designers, printers, and others involved in the project should always discuss any issues that might arise, such as job specifications and change orders. Where appropriate, designers should issue copies to all concerned parties in writing so that everyone is clear on how the project will be handled from start to finish.

When submitting a project to the printer, here is the information and material that you should provide:

- Contact (name and telephone number)
- Proofing contact (name and telephone number)
- Change order contact (name and telephone number)
- Job description
- Quantity
- Minimum quantity acceptable (no shortages)
- Overruns acceptable (billable)
- Paper
- Ink colors (CMYK, Pantone colors, special mixes, metallics)
- Ink drawdowns required (for critical specially mixed colors that must match sample swatches accurately)
- Varnishes (gloss, matte, dull)
- Letterpress (scoring, foiling, die-cutting)

- Trim size (finished size, flat size)
- Binding (folding, saddle stitching, perfect binding)
- Page count
- Bleeds
- Built-in blank pages
- CDs or disks containing clearly marked files
- Printout of the window or file directory showing disk contents
- Clear separated laser printouts of each page (one composite and one laser for each color CMYK plus additional colors)
- A copy of the print estimate to ensure that the printer is working with the correct cost data. Print estimates are often recalculated, so this keeps the designer and printer on the same page.

The Electronic Prepress Department

A DESIGNER'S BEST ALLIES IN PRODUCING high-quality work are usually chained to a computer in the heart of the print facility, nose-to-nose with their monitors. These folks comprise the electronic prepress department and they are your key contacts. Print reps are usually happy to direct you to the prepress department so you can question these specialists in-depth about specifications ranging from PDF settings, to hard-copy submissions, to registration and crop marks—just about any concern or question you might have. They will always help you, because in doing so, it makes their job easier. If you submit a clean job, they don't have to chase down missing fonts, corrupt images, or improperly saved files, and they won't have to redo anything because of incorrect specifications. They are the link between you and a clean, trouble-free printing experience, so take the time to get to know them.

Press Checks

Before the Press Check

- Discuss press check expectations and limitations carefully with your print rep.

- Be sure that you have allotted ample warning and travel time for scheduled press checks.

- Before you arrive, ensure that your printer has all the elements needed for your press check, such as swatches of specific colors, or samples of previously printed jobs to match.

- In addition to allowing for travel, be sure to schedule ample time for the press check itself. Many factors can play havoc with a printer's schedule: The job just before yours could go haywire and cause unexpected downtime; plates for your project could be faulty and require reimaging; or the power could go out. You name it, it's happened.

- If time is really tight, ask that your project be the first one run in the morning, or that it goes to press at night when you aren't occupied by other matters.

IT'S IMPORTANT TO FIND OUT IF THE printer is amenable to certain procedures, such as press checks. Good printers will encourage press checks because they appreciate the benefits of permitting a client to make final approvals before the press run begins. However, some printers are hesitant to allow press checks, either because they feel that the client may create confusion on press, or because they are mindful of lost production time while clients make last-minute decisions. While production time is a reasonable concern for the printer, you are better off taking your business to those who appreciate your needs—and your final approval—on press.

The most important thing every designer needs to bring to a press check is a Sharpie, or a similar felt-tipped pen. These are ideal for marking up press sheets, particularly on coated paper, because of their high visibility. Use a ballpoint pen and you might find yourself spending extra time hunting for all your notations.

It is highly recommended that all designers working with color invest in a good-quality loupe so they can review registration on proofs and press sheets during a press check. The magnifier can be adjusted to an individual's visual preferences.

In the first color press proof, you can see that the targets are in registration, but the reversed type in the image is off. In the second press proof, the image has been adjusted to register and the targets become unimportant.

Going to a Press Check

IF YOU ARE CONFIDENT that all bases have been covered, seeing your work in progress and being produced correctly will be a relief, and almost a formality. Good designers will come armed with either a written or mental list of elements to check on the proof.

A press check can be a terrifying experience for junior-level designers, who sometimes avoid signing off on press sheets for fear they will miss something that invokes wrath and shame when they return to the office. A press check is no place for a neophyte whose job may depend on making logical printing decisions. If you're working with a novice, do some handholding until they've gone to a few press checks with experienced designers. If *you* don't have much experience with press checks, tell your print rep. You can't fake it, and the first time you hold a solid-based magnifier, or *loupe*, upside down to inspect dots, every eye in the pressroom will roll. A good print rep or pressroom manager will guide you through the process, saving time for you and them. When creating a checklist, be sure to include the following:

1. Take out your Sharpie, and prepare to make notes—right on the press sheet.

2. Feel the paper first. Does it seem like the right weight? Then ask if the paper is what you specified. If you're the slightest bit concerned, or if the paper doesn't feel right, ask for the stock label. All paper comes labeled, whether it's in cartons or stacked on skids. Printers occasionally make human errors and load the wrong job stock for a press run. Make sure you're comfortable with the paper before proceeding.

3. Inspect the press sheet for overall appearance and color evenness. Look for hickeys, pinholes, and other blemishes.

4. Check for registration before looking through a loupe. Misregistration is usually noticeable first to the naked eye as off-color halos or rows of dots, particularly next to what should be crisp lines in images. Double-check questionable registration using the loupe.

5. Inspect the register *targets* on the press sheet for registration. Targets are just that—markings that let the press operator make registration adjustments before inspecting the images themselves for registration. Bear in mind that targets are often burned separately from other images, and due to minute variations in positioning the film against the plates, targets may be slightly off-register even though the images are dead on. By the same token, the targets can be registered perfectly, and the images may be off. Targets are a visual reference only.

6. Check for matches of specially mixed colors against your sample swatches or color guide.

7. Scan the press sheet for content, missing images, anything that doesn't look right.

8. Next, compare the proofs for each individual page to the corresponding press sheets for color breaks and color accuracy, and to ensure that any changes you requested in the proofing stage have been made.

9. When you're done, ask the press operator if they've had a press sheet *ruled up*. Here, the operator uses a T-square on a light table to draw lines connecting the trim marks, ensuring that the trims don't cut off critical elements. If this hasn't been done, you're within your rights to ask for it.

10. Pick a convenient corner of the press sheet you just marked up and label it "1."

11. Discuss any needed adjustments with the press operator or pressroom manager. Unless you see something that is clearly out of whack, such as a missing image, go over your adjustments all at once. You'll drive the press operator crazy if you ask for a dozen changes to be made one at a time, each requiring a separate press startup.

12. From this point on, you'll be whittling down your concerns to acceptable levels through a successive series of adjustments. Good print quality is extremely subjective, and you may ask the press operator to make a half-dozen series of corrections before you're satisfied that what you see on the sheet is as good as it will get.

13. When you are satisfied that the job is satisfactory, and that your client will accept it, sign and date the sheet and ask for two or three press sheets from the same pull.

Press sheets on the press
table and ready for inspection.
Here's where your Sharpie
comes in handy for making
notations directly onto
the sheet.

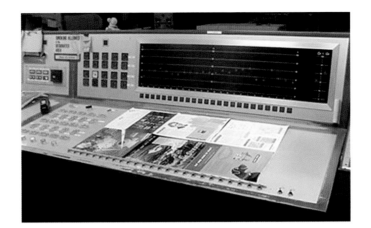

Pressrooms can be filled with
activity, noise, and fast-moving
machinery, which can add to
the anxiety of a press check for
the novice. Experienced help is
the best cure.

At press checks, you should
view press sheets with
corrected lighting, either on
a press table or in a viewing
booth, such as the one
shown here.

Here, the press operator adjusts color and registration with electronic push pads connected to the press.

A loupe provides a clear and accurate view of registration. It can be a worthwhile investment for designers who frequently attend press checks.

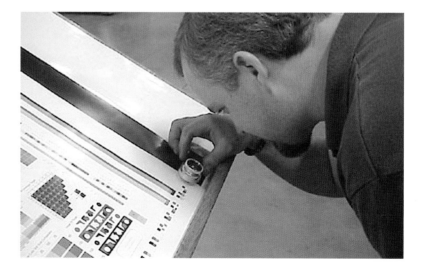

Each time you ask for press adjustments and a new sheet to review, the press operator must start the press and print several dozen sheets to achieve correct operating balances. By asking for all of your registration and color adjustments at the same time, you'll save time and paper.

147
...

Working
with Your
Printer

Knowing When to Say When

EXPERIENCE CAN'T BE TAUGHT. If you've established a reasonable rapport with your print rep, have faith in your choice of printers, and believe they are doing everything they can to make your job look as good as possible, you should be comfortable following their lead and accepting their advice during press checks. At times, you'll be asked to sign off on a press sheet with assurances that your adjustments will be made before the press run begins.

Presses are more sensitive to operating conditions than many people realize. Most require a few minutes running time to stabilize ink/water balances, to achieve optimum operating temperatures, and for ink tack to stabilize through the roller systems. A press operator's nightmare is a job that must be started and stopped repeatedly, but this is the condition under which press checks are conducted. The operator may tell you that they have to get the press running to stabilize the process, or need to perform some time-consuming maintenance procedure before the job can begin. If you've chosen your printer with care, and trust your own judgment, take them at their word and let them do their job.

If you've given your work to a printer who low-balled the bid, they may want to get you out the door as quickly as possible so they can run the press and make up for some of the low bid price. As a ploy to get you to sign off, they may also tell you that they've got to get the press running, but first need to perform maintenance procedures. If you don't quite believe them, sign off on the press sheet with a note about conditions that they've promised to correct, and ask for extra samples.

Avoiding Nightmare Scenarios

AT ONE TIME OR ANOTHER, every graphic designer will have—or hear about—a color printing nightmare. To keep these to a minimum, good designers carefully select their printer, clearly communicate their needs and concerns, and pay attention to detail. Many printing jobs cost as much as new car, but some designers spend more time on the auto lot than they do shopping for a good printer.

One way to avoid color conflict is to run sample proofs of your images. In this example, a designer thought this photo was the correct shade of burgundy. After seeing the printer's press proof, they realized that what appeared to be burgundy on the computer screen was extremely pink in print. The image and press proof had to be redone.

Dust and scratches in the sky didn't raise red flags at the proofing stage, and were exaggerated even more on press. It was a costly error: Because the image was critical to the client's brochure, the job was pulled from press and the photo retouched.

Color variations on a press run can result in varying samples as shown by these images. It's usually a judgment call, but in this case, the image was not critical enough to warrant a reprint.

Eight Steps toward Trouble-free Printing

Value is seldom reflected in the lowest bid, and an extremely low bid on a complicated project should trigger a warning. Investigate low bids thoroughly before committing your project. Hidden costs in the form of change orders can bite you, or your high-end annual report could be farmed out to a low-quality printer in Timbuktu. Make certain that your print reps are quoting on the same specifications. Some printers have been known to print a portion of sample-quality material on the premium stock specified, and run the balance of the job on a lower-grade paper. Check your printer's references. What follows are a few reminders of what you need to remember to avoid turning a dream job into a nightmare.

1. **SPECIFICATIONS**

   Make certain your specifications are clear and concise and that your print rep understands them completely. Ask questions: Will it need scoring? Should it be varnished to avoid scuffing? Is the specified paper a good choice for the project?

2. **COLOR MATCHING**

   If specially mixed ink colors *must* accurately match a color swatch or sample, you should make this clear in your specifications and to your print rep. You can request ink draw down samples on the same paper as your job specifies. Remember that color guides will fade with age and that minor variations occur from one guide to another.

3. **PRESS CHECKS**

   If you want to see your job on press, make sure you have that option. In some print shops, you can ensure a higher standard of work if they know the job will be press checked and that you will have a copy of the signed-off press sheet when samples are delivered.

4. **PRESS PROOFS**

   If you've signed off on an initial press check and are comfortable having the printer handle the remainder, ask that the pressroom manager or sales rep sign off on the runs. Ask for sample press sheets of each run.

5. **PAPER**

   When press checking, always verify that the paper used for the press check and press run is the stock you specified. If you sign off on a press sheet and the stock is not the right weight or grade, some printers will insist that it's your fault for okaying the wrong paper. It's not unreasonable to ask for verification of stock at the press check.

6. **SAMPLES**

   Always ask for samples. Many ask for ten to twenty samples, which are easy to handpick out of the run. Some print buyers ask for fifty samples, which are much more difficult to pick out of an erratic press run. If you have the slightest concerns about the printer you're using for a project, ask for fifty on your specification sheet. This number will probably count as part of the overall delivery quantity on the job, but it gives you a better reflection of the quality of the run.

7. **PAPER AND REGISTRATION ON PRESS**

   Printing on a large press with heavy ink coverage and small reversed images on light paper can often result in a disappointing finished product. Good registration is a key to good presswork, but there are inherent limitations when you have a flimsy 38-inch wide sheet of paper traveling through six units of a multicolor printing press.

   If you're planning a potentially difficult project, grill your print rep about their press capacities. Direct-to-plate printing provides more-accurate registration from color to color because the variables of film—and the steps required to expose printing plates—have been eliminated. Film isn't as stable as the aluminum compounds used to make a plate, and the latter's stability generally enables more accurate registration. This is a good point to remember when you're going out for bids.

8. **FINANCIAL IMPLICATIONS OF COLOR MISTAKES**

   This is a touchy subject that all printers and designers have to endure at some point in their career. Plainly said, color mistakes are costly. The best way to avoid color mistakes is awareness. Run a color sample with your printer and show it to your client. If there are any changes to be made, now is the time to do it—not after the job has printed.

Printing through the Ages

Printing became a "high-volume" industry in the fifteenth century with Johannes Gutenberg's introduction of moveable type. This woodcut illustrates the same basic principles we use today. On the left foreground, the typesetter is at work, with the proofreader next to him. In the center foreground, the printer's devil, usually a young boy, is stacking freshly printed sheets, while the printer pulls the screw handle to create an impression on the wooden press. Behind the printer, a woman sews the binding on finished books, and in the background, the deliveryman is on the way out the door. And of course, on the far right is the shop owner, probably asking why this is all taking so long. A full day's work in this era would produce about three hundred printed sheets.

In another fifteenth century woodcut, the printer in the background on the left is holding a leather-covered inkpad, which is used to tap ink onto the type. This was the earliest form of ink-density control, and took years to master. The printer's helper uses a long handle on the vise screw to press the impression block onto a sheet of paper. On the left, a typesetter uses an opened book as copy to set type.

Like modern printing presses, early models were built with massive beams to distribute the pressures required to print a single sheet of paper. This press has an advanced design for its time, with metal screw vise and leverage handle for applying printing pressure by hand.

SUMMARY

THE VALUE OF HELPING CLIENTELE make good printer choices should never be underestimated. Understanding the printing options that are available today, and knowing the processes that your printers use can quickly lead you to the most effective vendors, and result in a final product that will meet your expectations. Digital imaging and direct-to-press processes have created many opportunities for short press runs that would be cost prohibitive using traditional lithographic techniques. This is a growing market and is ripe for designers who guide their clientele into taking full advantage of new technologies.

156
...

GRAPHIC
DESIGNER'S
COLOR
HANDBOOK

COLORFUL WORDS FROM THE PRESSROOM

DESIGNERS AND PRINT PROFESSIONALS HAVE A SYMBIOTIC RELATIONSHIP. Each expects the other to hold to the highest standards, and each knows that their success hinges on the other. It's an important concept to understand when working through the color process.

Any designer fortunate enough to establish a solid working relationship with their printer often becomes privy to the facility's inner workings. A personal tour of the press and prepress areas is an invaluable experience, and all designers should try it at least once in their careers. In addition to giving you a better understanding of color mechanics, it also provides insight into how colors work together on screen and on press. The color brochure concept that you sketched out on a notepad will suddenly become very real as a press operator pulls a sheet off the press and hands it you. with this in mind, you should strive to understand the realities of print production.

What Printers Look for in Color Submissions

IN CHAPTER 4, WE DISCUSSED the information and materials that designers should submit along with their print jobs. Here, we'll delve into the practical aspects of offset print production by covering situations that often arise on the press floor. Many of these situations have the potential to affect your designs, and understanding them will help to clarify the limitations of print production.

One of the most common mistakes that designers make when submitting art is failing to convert all images from RGB to CMYK. If you don't do it, your printer may not be able to, and the images probably won't print.

158
...

GRAPHIC
DESIGNER'S
COLOR
HANDBOOK

Common Mistakes

EVERYONE MAKES MISTAKES, and designers and printers are no exception. However, when the errors add up, a seemingly simple job can quickly turn into a nightmare. Ask a printer about the common mistakes made by designers, and they'll probably cite unconverted RGB images, missing fonts and files, and miscommunication. Avoiding these mistakes is especially important when color is involved because the stakes are much higher. Color corrections at press are costly and time-consuming, and they tend to make everyone crabby.

23 23 23

Extremely tight trimming
requirements often pose problems, and can be difficult to
overcome. It's relatively easy
to design an element—such as
the folio on top—that depends
on precise trimming. The next
three figures show how page
layout, press registration,
folding, and trimming can
cause unwanted variations.

Common mistakes:

- Wrong, missing, or corrupt fonts
- Missing images and files
- Renaming TIF or EPS files, which will break the link with the page layout file
- Images and files improperly saved
- RGB or indexed color files not converted to CMYK
- Text or images too close to the trim
- Position-only images still in the final file
- Missing or incorrect lasers copies
- Corrupt files
- Missing contact information
- Incorrect trim size
- Incorrect imposition

The best way to avoid mistakes is to communicate effectively with your printer. If
you ask all the necessary color questions
and run sample proofs early in the project, you will avoid conflict later. Don't
ever be afraid to ask questions, no matter
how inane they may sound. When working with color, leave no stone unturned.
You don't want to risk losing a client
because of poor color performance.

When Things Go Horribly Pink

PRINTING CONSIDERATIONS loom large from the moment you begin designing a color project. You can spend all day tweaking your colors, but the effort will be useless if they don't translate on press. Never hesitate to run proofs, especially if the images are questionable. It takes only one bad image to spoil a project.

A good printer will alert you about poor color choices. You might be tempted to disagree, but printers have the best understanding of how the colors will translate into a finished product. If the printer thinks your choices are wrong, and you're inclined to stick to your guns, get a second opinion from a comparable source.

Duotone Effects and Expectations

IF YOUR COLOR PROJECT includes black-and-white photos, you might consider dressing them up by converting them to *duotones*, *tritones*, or *quadtones*. Here, the photo is reproduced using two, three, or four colors respectively, adding depth and vibrance to an otherwise lackluster image. Many variables come into play when producing such images, and printers often prefer scanning them inhouse. Printers usually have common protocols for multitone production that work well with their systems.

Because quadtones are reproduced in all four process colors, they will reflect any color shifts on press. If you're running them with four-color images that are being pushed in a certain color direction—such as by adding cyan or magenta—the quadtones will reflect the same color cast. However, with many images, this can be pleasing to the eye, and shouldn't be cause for alarm.

Roll the Presses

NUMEROUS PHYSICAL and mechanical considerations affect every job on press. Some are out of your control, with one possible exception: Your choice of printers. Still, designers who understand such elements as ink density, sheet layouts, and signature formats will develop a knack for envisioning the project as it will appear on the press sheet.

Pressroom Controls

ALTHOUGH THERE ARE FEW industry standards that compel individual printing companies to perform in a predetermined fashion, manufacturers of proofing and control systems offer equipment that is carefully evaluated to meet industry expectations. Offset presses, as massive and ominous-looking as they may be, are relatively sensitive machines that operate with incredibly close tolerances. Settings that are off by a few thousandths of an inch can have detrimental effects on print quality. No two presses operate exactly alike. Regular maintenance, the use of *test forms*, and proper understanding of color bars and densitometer readings are essential when producing high-quality color.

162
...
GRAPHIC
DESIGNER'S
COLOR
HANDBOOK

Duotones are often used in two-color print projects, providing an inexpensive way to add color to black-and-white images.

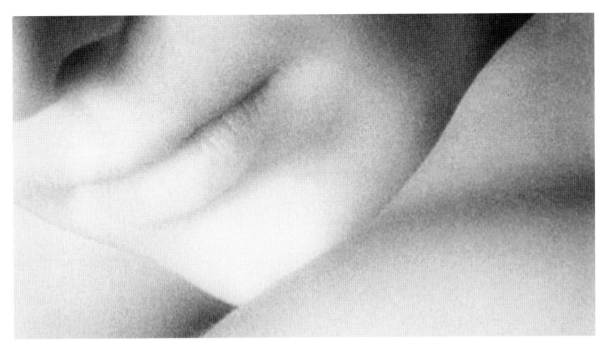

163
...
Colorful
Words
from the
Pressroom

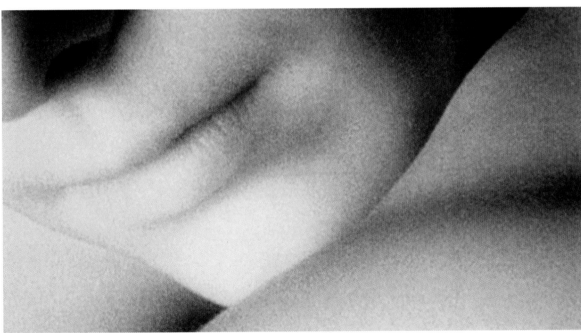

Tritones, like quadtones, can add color and warmth to the page. This tritone consists of a full black-and-white halftone with small percentages of cyan and magenta added to midtones and highlights.

Handheld reflection densitometers are invaluable for monitoring press runs and maintaining press calibrations. Designers should be aware of this procedure when working with press operators. (Courtesy Heidelberg USA, Inc.)

Densitometers

A *DENSITOMETER* IS (usually) a handheld electronic device that measures ink density, dot size, dot gain, *ink trap* (the ability of one ink color to print, or *trap*, over another), and hue error and grayness. Transmission densitometers are designed to read through transparent material, such as film. However, most pressrooms use reflection densitometers, which bounce a light beam from the surface of a sheet and electronically calculate the result. In most color jobs, these measurements are taken on color bars printed outside the image area.

Ink Density

INK DENSITY REFERS to the amount of each ink color applied to the press sheet. More ink results in higher densities and a corresponding increase in the depth of color. When you tell the press operator you would like to see more blue in a particular image, they increase the cyan ink flow with electronic or manual adjustments, then pull another set of press sheets for your inspection. Invariably, they will check ink density with a densitometer before and after making the adjustment, the latter to ensure that you haven't exceeded optimal levels or thrown overall color out of balance.

165
...

Colorful
Words
from the
Pressroom

In the first illustration, the
sky looks a little washed out.
Adding cyan on press will
make the sky bluer and
brighter, but it also increases
the blue in the entire image.
Unlike photo-editing programs,
such as Adobe Photoshop,
offset presses cannot make
selective adjustments within
the confines of an image.

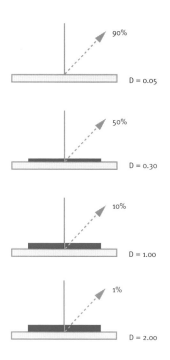

90%
D = 0.05

50%
D = 0.30

10%
D = 1.00

1%
D = 2.00

166
...

GRAPHIC
DESIGNER'S
COLOR
HANDBOOK

How Densitometers Work— A Short Primer

A REFLECTION DENSITOMETER, as noted earlier, bounces light from a controlled internal source to the surface of a printed sheet, and back into a series of filters and monitors that translate the reflection into numeric values. An increase in ink results in a correspondingly higher reading. The readings of each process color, taken from the color bar on your approved press sheet, will help the press operator maintain optimal settings throughout the print run. This can be a balancing act. Overly light density will increase the number of hickeys, because thinner ink is also sticky. If the density is too high, you'll see increased dot gain, plugged shadows, and perhaps set-off onto subsequent press sheets. Between these extremes, the operator can use ink adjustments to create wide variations in color output.

You can use your eye to evaluate ink density, but you'll get more accurate results using a reflection densitometer. This device can detect slight variations in ink density and helps the press operator log and maintain the densities that you approved.

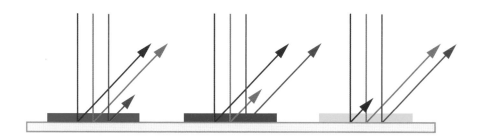

This illustration shows a simplified view of the inner workings of a reflection densitometer. Light is reflected from ink and paper into a series of filters and sensors that translate the signal into numeric values.

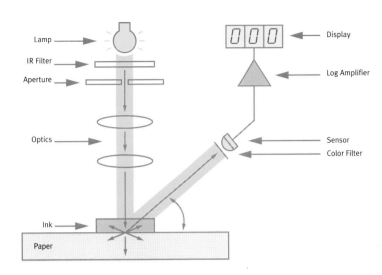

Components of a Reflection Densitometer

Reflection densitometers are sensitive to such subtleties as the shadow the ink dot casts inside the paper. Minute variations can be measured, notated, and stored to allow repeatable results on reprints.

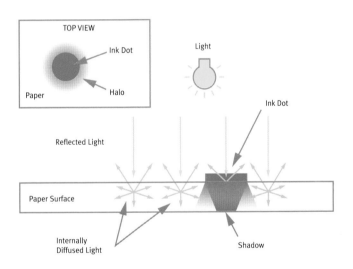

The Effect of Light Scattering Properties

168
...

**GRAPHIC
DESIGNER'S
COLOR
HANDBOOK**

Handheld reflection densitometers, as seen in this exploded
view of spreading dots, can
detect changes in screen
values more accurately than
the naked eye.

Densitometers and Screen Values

DENSITOMETERS ALSO TRANSLATE
screen values numerically. By monitoring the screen values in color bars, the
press operator can detect variations
that may affect the system's operating
balances. With ink densities on the high
side, shadows may gradually begin to
fill in, creating unacceptable dot gain.
Changes in ink/water balance will also
affect screen values.

Densitometers and Ink Trap

THE TERM *TRAP* SERVES DUAL purposes in the pressroom. "Image trapping" refers to how images are overlaid
on the press sheet. "Ink trapping" refers
to printing one color of ink over another;
bad trapping results in poor dot reproduction and lost color gamut. Under
ideal conditions, with proper ink tacks
and ink/water balances, colors will
smoothly print over each other. With
improperly tacked inks or other problems, overprinting can become mottled
and uneven. Good ink trap is imperative
for high-quality printing. The illustration
shows blocks of solid ink overprint that
are large enough to see, but the same
thing is happening to the tiny dots in
your four-color job.

169
...

Colorful
Words
from the
Pressroom

This series of color blocks depicts ink that is trapping (overprinting) as it should be, and the effect is a smooth color. The combination of 100 percent yellow and 100 percent red looks just like it was intended—solid red. In the green block, 100 percent cyan overprinted by 100 percent yellow produces a smooth green. Good ink trapping is a key to good printing.

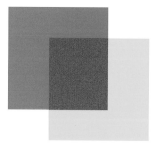

These blocks illustrate the effects of poor ink trap. The yellow is not trapping over the red properly, producing a mottled-looking green. And it's not trapping well over the cyan, with similar results. All of these blocks represent poor ink trap. The cure is to adjust press balances or ink tacks.

171
...
Colorful
Words
from the
Pressroom

Good color printers invest in high-quality equipment, rigorous maintenance programs, and quality materials that add up to excellent reproduction, as seen in the first image. The second image shows what you can expect from an inexpensive facility with poorly maintained equipment.

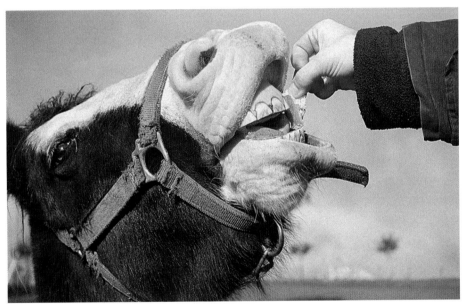

Why Bad Traps Happen on Good Presses

THE WHY'S AND HOW'S of ink trapping could probably fill a book. What follows is a practical overview.

Ink Quality

INK QUALITY PLAYS A ROLE in trapping problems. Cheap inks can be overly sensitive to press variations and can fluctuate radically during a print run.

Good-quality ink handles the printing process with relative ease. High-end printers tend to buy grades of ink that offer consistent handling characteristics on press.

Press Roller Systems—A Major Player

INKING SYSTEMS ON PRINTING presses are designed to distribute ink smoothly and evenly to the plate, and from there to the blanket and onto your press sheet. Inking rollers are made of steel cores covered with specially formulated rubber compounds that are ground to specific diameters. When the rubber rollers are new, they have a soft velvety surface that is ideal for transferring thin ink films. As rollers age, the surfaces tend to swell and harden, and sometimes develop cracks and pits. Their ability to transfer ink diminishes, and print quality suffers. Effective press roller life can range from two to six months, depending on the chemicals used to clean them, roller adjustments, and shop environment.

Just as car tires can be retreaded, press rollers can be recovered with new rubber and given new life. This is a common practice, and several companies specialize in remanufacturing printing rollers. Many printers maintain a regular roller exchange program, but unfortunately, some don't.

At rest, press-inking rollers are raised from the plate cylinder, as shown at the top in this cutaway side view. When the press is turned on and printing, rollers are mechanically lowered onto the plate.

Keeping New Rubber on the Press

MAINTAINING A REGULAR ROLLER exchange program is expensive and can be a significant part of a shop's overhead. The best printers adhere to a regular exchange of press rollers and factor this into their production costs. Others put off exchanging rollers as long as possible. This can be reflected in lower costs, but is also reflected in lower-quality color work.

How Important Can Rollers Really Be?

A THIRTY-YEAR-OLD PRINTING PRESS in reasonable condition with good press rollers will print better than a year-old press with aged rollers. Many printing problems attributed to mechanical glitches have been cured with roller replacements.

Press *form rollers*, which physically contact the plate, can be lowered by hand to reveal the stripes on the printing plate. This figure illustrates the proper appearance of stripes in a press's magenta printing unit. These stripes can be measured, and their widths adjusted to the press manufacturer's specifications.

This figure illustrates ink stripes of aged, poorly adjusted press rollers. The stripe at the top results from a form roller adjusted too tightly to the plate cylinder. The second stripe shows the effect of a roller swollen in the center. The third stripe is unevenly adjusted from one side to the other. The bottom stripe is adjusted too lightly to the plate cylinder. These problems indicate poor adjustments, poor roller condition, or a combination of the two. All will lead to poor print reproduction.

Smooth Solids
on Press

174
...

GRAPHIC
DESIGNER'S
COLOR
HANDBOOK

PRINTING SMOOTH SOLIDS ON offset presses is one of a press operator's greatest challenges. Good inking rollers, coupled with a high-end press, make solid reproduction a relatively trouble-free operation. Poor inking rollers, and often the less expensive presses on the market, can turn solids into an operator's nightmare. Great solids don't come cheap, and if you've got solids in your design, you'll want to take a close look at the capacities of your low bidders.

A proof should give you a good representation of the image you'll see on press, as illustrated here.

Mechanical Ghosting

MECHANICAL GHOSTING REFERS TO artifacts that appear when solid or screened images are disrupted by design elements that break the even distribution of ink. This always occurs in the direction the sheet travels. You end up with slight variations in ink density in areas where you want even coverage. Mechanical ghosting is a fact of life to some degree. Projects with a high likelihood of mechanical ghosting are best printed on high-quality presses in good operating condition.

Here are two examples of solids you'll see reproduced on low-end presses, or expensive models with aging, misadjusted rollers.

176
...

GRAPHIC
DESIGNER'S
COLOR
HANDBOOK

FDA

The Nation's Premier
Consumer Protection And
Health Agency

U.S. Food and Drug Administration
5600 Fishers Lane
Rockville, MD 20857

1-888-INFO-FDA
www.fda.gov

U.S. DEPARTMENT OF HEALTH AND HUMAN SERVICES
DHHS Publication No. (FDA) 01-1316

These images show the effect
of mechanical ghosting. The
first image, a proof with an
even, solid background, shows
no ghosting. The second image
illustrates mechanical ghosting
on an inexpensive press, with
a noticeable difference in ink
density following the edges of
images that break up the solid
coverage. The third image is
printed on a high-end press
designed for demanding jobs.

177
...

Colorful

Words

from the

Pressroom

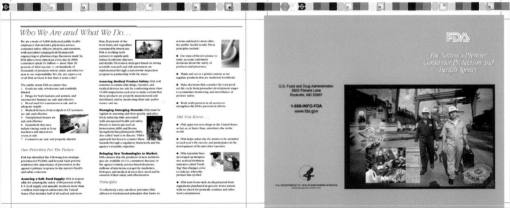

Duplicator presses are common in small and quick print shops. These machines can handle sheet sizes up to 11 x 17 inches and do an excellent job of reproducing relatively simple color projects. Most have only two inking form rollers, as shown in this illustration, and are not designed to handle large, solid images.

Small duplicating presses are not designed to print the heavy solids seen here. The arrow shows the direction of sheet traveling through the press.

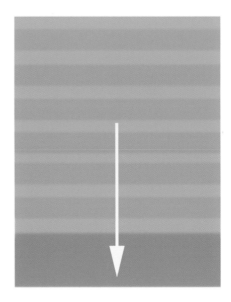

Test Forms for Offset Printing

GOOD PRINTERS FREQUENTLY RUN TEST FORMS—such as those provided by the Graphic Arts Technical Foundation (GATF)—to monitor print quality of the presses they operate. These exacting forms offer common reference points for evaluating virtually every aspect of offset printing, including dot gain, ink trapping, color fidelity, color gamut, and the accuracy of *print length*. Print length is a measurement of the printed image from the leading edge to the tail edge of the press sheet.

By printing the test forms from digital files and then submitting them to the GATF for evaluation, printers gain a valuable means of maintaining quality control on their equipment. If your printer uses these forms, or similarly rigorous process controls, it's a good sign that they take their work seriously. Many printers simply wing it, hope for the best, and then blame any quality problems that arise on everything except their process controls.

GATF Test Forms

WE HAVE INCLUDED ON THE FOLLOWING PAGES a series of test form elements provided by the GATF. These forms and their results tend to stay tucked away within the printing industry, but they are highly informative and deserve recognition for the positive impact they have on the quality control of high end color reproduction.

Elements of these test forms are appropriate to the digital printing process, and will give you an idea of the demanding definition and color fidelity that high quality printers are striving to achieve.

THE GATF TEST FORMS shown here illustrate the steps that better printing companies take to ensure quality. Each form presents difficult challenges for offset reproduction, pushing the presses to their limits.

180
...

GRAPHIC
DESIGNER'S
COLOR
HANDBOOK

Low-key images

The red couch photograph is referred to as a *low-key* image because of the predominance of dark hues in the midtone to shadow portions. This photograph also presents a challenge in its high level of resolved detail. (Courtesy GATF)

High-key images

The wedding photograph is referred to as *high key* because the dominant tones are light pastels and whites, which fall in the highlight to midtone areas. (Courtesy GATF)

Realistic skin tones

In the painting kids photograph, the challenge is to reproduce all five skin tones equally well. (Courtesy GATF)

Capturing tonal differences

In this portrait, close attention is required to capture tonal differences in the face, chest, arms, and hands, as well as more subtle transitions from the forehead, cheeks, nose, and chin. (Courtesy GATF)

Measuring color cast

This photo, dominated by tones approximating neutral grays, provides a good measure of color cast. The image is also low key due to the preponderance of dark tones and relatively few highlights. (Courtesy GATF)

Broad color gamuts

This photo provides a broad color gamut. The fruit and fabrics were selected for their variety of saturated hues, pushing the limits of transparency film. Reproduction of these hues is particularly difficult. (Courtesy GATF)

182
...

**GRAPHIC
DESIGNER'S
COLOR
HANDBOOK**

This photo of a covered bridge demonstrates the reproduction of *memory colors*. As the name implies, these are colors, such as green grass and blue sky, that the viewer subconsciously compares with their own expectations based on what they've seen before. (Courtesy GATF)

Twenty-two step tone scales show each process color, plus blue, green, red, and an even mix of cyan, magenta, and yellow. (Courtesy GATF)

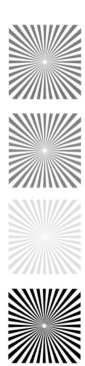

	C	M	Y	K	R	G	B	3C
5								
10								
15								
20								
25								
30								
35								
40								
45								
50								
55								
60								
65								
70								
75								
80								
85								
90								
95								
S								

Star targets indicate the resolution and directional bias of an imaging system. Systems capable of higher resolution will come closer to presenting the center of the star as a single point. (Courtesy GATF)

183
...
Colorful
Words
from the
Pressroom

The line-resolution target shows the system's ability to handle positive and reversed line elements and a variety of orientations. (Courtesy GATF)

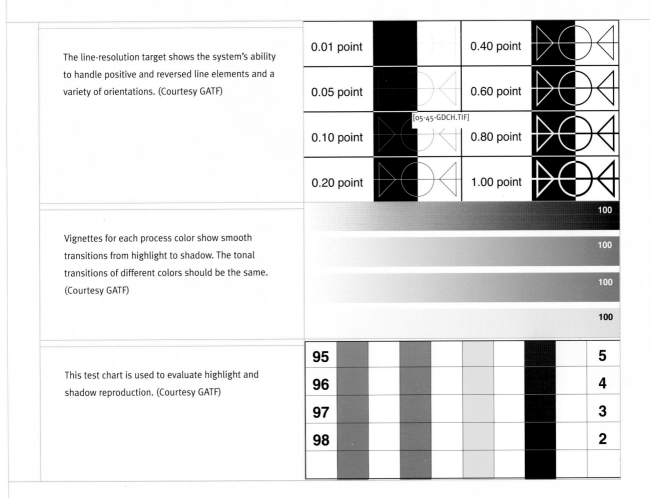

Vignettes for each process color show smooth transitions from highlight to shadow. The tonal transitions of different colors should be the same. (Courtesy GATF)

This test chart is used to evaluate highlight and shadow reproduction. (Courtesy GATF)

These gray values are recommended for reproducing neutrals with typical magazine production techniques and materials. (Courtesy GATF)

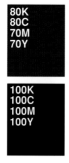

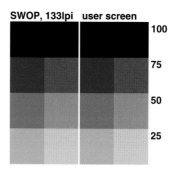

These pixel line patterns are sensitive targets for high-exposure imaging systems. (Courtesy GATF)

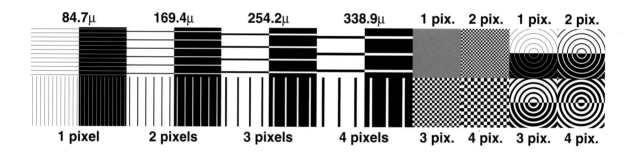

The image fit target is used to evaluate the register accuracy of any output device. Elements are placed with no trapping between colors. (Courtesy GATF)

Type Resolution Target / D-Max Patches

The type resolution target has samples of type ranging from 24 points to one point in positive and reversed formats. Most systems do not resolve positive and negative one-point type successfully. (Courtesy GATF)

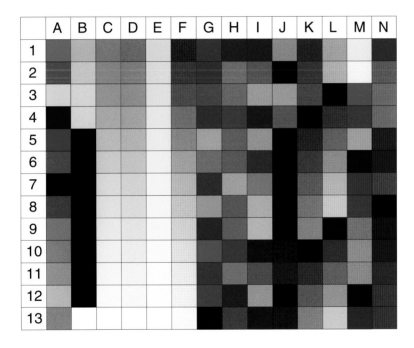

The colors in this data set were chosen to demonstrate the color gamut of the imaging system. (Courtesy GATF)

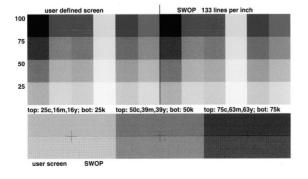

The GCA/GATF digital proof comparator contains 25, 50, 75, and 100 percent tone values to show how the system reproduces process colors, plus blue, green, and red. The black tone patches provide a visual reference against which you can compare the neutrality of the three-color patches. (Courtesy GATF)

Tones in these opposed line targets should be uniform, with no differences between tones formed by the horizontal and vertical lines.
(Courtesy GATF)

The color control bar consists of a sequence of 100, 75, 50, and 25 percent tone patches in cyan, magenta, yellow, black, blue, green, and red. This confirms that the imaging system is producing consistent color and tone from page to page.
(Courtesy GATF)

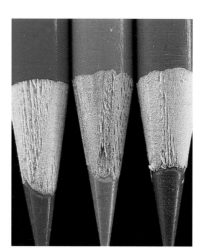

This photo presents significant areas of highly saturated blue, red, and green that help define the saturation limits of the reproduction system. Also, the slightly off-neutral hues of the pencil tips are highly suscepti-ble to color variations.
(Courtesy GATF)

The gray balance charts help determine the best combination of cyan, magenta, and yellow needed to reproduce a neutral scale. Operators usually evaluate gray visually and must do so under standard viewing conditions. (Courtesy GATF)

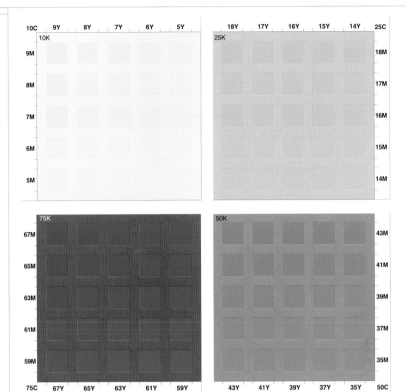

The process color tint blocks are used to evaluate the uniformity of an even dot pattern. Additionally, the tint patches will also change value if dot gain is adjusted. (Courtesy GATF)

This portrait of a young woman in front of an abstract colored background provides a human image to evaluate. Because fleshtones are so familiar to us, we're very critical of how hue and contrast are reproduced. (Courtesy GATF)

Press Sheet Configurations

PRESS SHEETS ARE SET UP TO RUN on a variety of press sizes. Small duplicating presses are generally built to handle 8 ½ x 11 to 12 x 18-inch sheet sizes. The next size up is 14 x 20 inches. Half-size presses fall in the 20 x 26-inch range. The next most common size press handles a 28 x 40-inch sheet. While press sizes can go up to a whopping 70 inches, the vast majority fall into these ranges.

Signature Sizes

PRESSES ALSO HANDLE A RANGE of potential *signature* sizes. A signature is a printed press sheet designed to fold at least once to become part of a publication. Signatures are generally multiples of four pages—one sheet folded in half—and signature page counts rise in four-page increments. Trim sizes for finished publications run a wide range, from tiny 3 x 5's up to 11 x 14 and larger. Most common publications fall within the 5 ½ x 8 ½ to 8 ½ x 11-inch sizes.

These images show the sheet direction through an offset press. Duplicating presses feed an 8 ½ x 11-inch sheet on the 8 ½-inch side. Larger presses invariably feed paper on the long side, as illustrated here with a 19 x 25-inch sheet and a 25 x 38-inch sheet.

All sheetfed presses require a gripper edge and set-back, which constitute a no-print zone before the printing image begins. (This no-print zone is usually minimum of a ½ inch.)

Back	Front
8	1
2	7
6	3
4	5

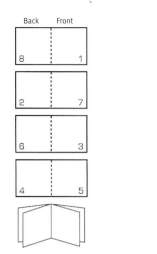

Back	Front
12	1
2	11
10	3

Back	Front
4	9
8	5
6	7

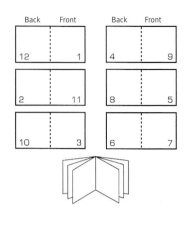

Back	Front
16	1
2	15
14	3
4	13

B	Front
12	5
6	11
10	7
8	9

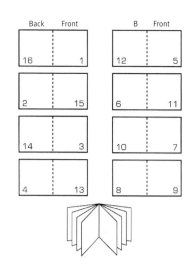

Back	Front
20	1
2	19
18	3
4	17
16	5

Back	Front
6	15
14	7
8	13
12	9
10	11

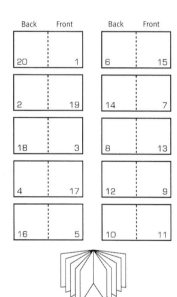

Back	Front
28	1
2	27
26	3
4	25
24	5
6	23
22	7

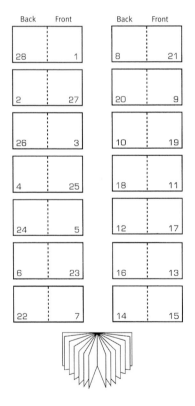

Back	Front
8	21
20	9
10	19
18	11
12	17
16	13
14	15

Back	Front
32	1
2	31
30	3
4	29
28	5
6	27
26	7
8	25

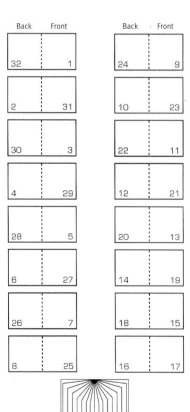

Back	Front
24	9
10	23
22	11
12	21
20	13
14	19
18	15
16	17

Common signature sizes.

Layouts and Imposition Dummies

UNDERSTANDING IMPOSITION and layout dummies is a key to effective design and predictable output. These are often nothing more than a piece of letter-sized paper folded in half for a four-page dummy, in quarters for an eight-page dummy, or in eighths for a sixteen-page dummy. With page numbers noted consecutively, the sheet can be unfolded to reveal the pages that will fall on each side of a press sheet. These *printer spreads* are much different from *reader spreads*, and they will vary from printer to printer depending on press sizes and how their bindery equipment is configured for folding.

Seeing a dummy layout of your job can greatly help in making color decisions. If you are running a variety of Pantone spot colors, you can set them up to print on pages on one side of the press sheet, thus avoiding extra passes through the press, extra plates, and extra press washes to change colors.

Dummy layouts can also help you anticipate potential problems, such as mechanical ghosting, and they let you see the placement of critical color images that you may need to adjust on press.

Your print rep should be able to supply you with a variety of imposition dummies and press sheet layout configurations as illustrated. Imposition dummies can vary from shop to shop, depending on press sizes and folding equipment.

This illustration shows a typical four-page layout dummy, followed by an example of how it would appear on press. The blue lines represent non-printing trim lines, while the red line represents the non-printing fold line.

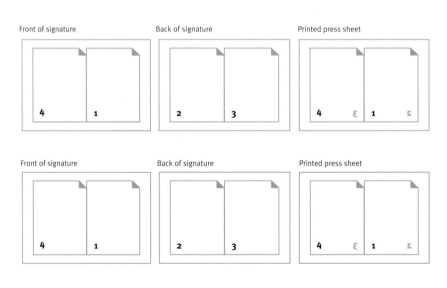

Front of signature Back of signature Printed press sheet

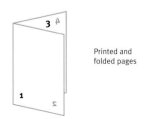

Printed and folded pages

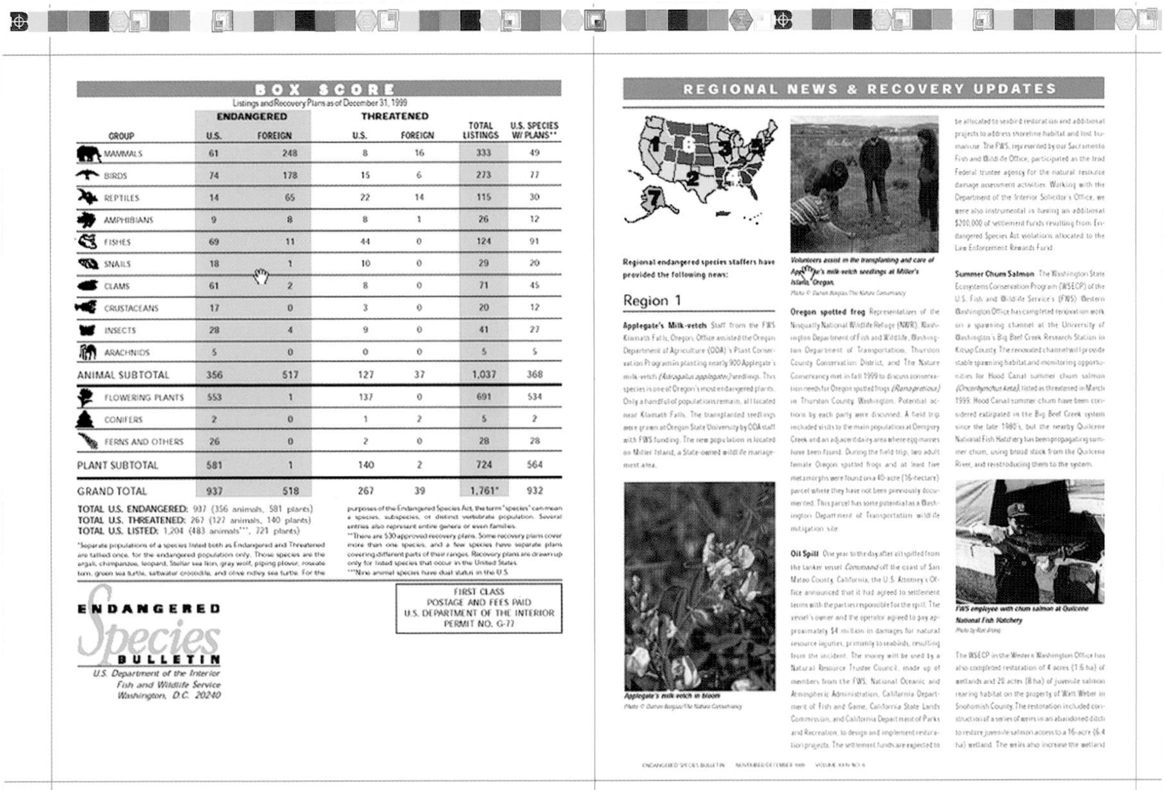

191
...
Colorful
Words
from the
Pressroom

BOX SCORE
Listings and Recovery Plans as of December 31, 1999

GROUP	ENDANGERED		THREATENED		TOTAL LISTINGS	U.S. SPECIES W/ PLANS**
	U.S.	FOREIGN	U.S.	FOREIGN		
MAMMALS	61	248	8	16	333	49
BIRDS	74	178	15	6	273	77
REPTILES	14	65	22	14	115	30
AMPHIBIANS	9	8	8	1	26	12
FISHES	69	11	44	0	124	91
SNAILS	18	1	10	0	29	20
CLAMS	61	2	8	0	71	45
CRUSTACEANS	17	0	3	0	20	12
INSECTS	28	4	9	0	41	27
ARACHNIDS	5	0	0	0	5	5
ANIMAL SUBTOTAL	356	517	127	37	1,037	368
FLOWERING PLANTS	553	1	137	0	691	534
CONIFERS	2	0	1	2	5	2
FERNS AND OTHERS	26	0	2	0	28	28
PLANT SUBTOTAL	581	1	140	2	724	564
GRAND TOTAL	937	518	267	39	1,761*	932

TOTAL U.S. ENDANGERED: 937 (356 animals, 581 plants)
TOTAL U.S. THREATENED: 267 (127 animals, 140 plants)
TOTAL U.S. LISTED: 1,204 (483 animals***, 721 plants)

*Separate populations of a species listed both as Endangered and Threatened are tallied once. For the endangered population only. Those species are the argali, chimpanzee, leopard, Stellar sea lion, gray wolf, piping plover, roseate tern, green sea turtle, saltwater crocodile, and olive ridley sea turtle. For the

purposes of the Endangered Species Act, the term "species" can mean a species, subspecies, or distinct vertebrate population. Several entries also represent entire genera or even families.
**There are 530 approved recovery plans. Some recovery plans cover more than one species, and a few species have separate plans covering different parts of their ranges. Recovery plans are drawn up only for listed species that occur in the United States.
***Nine animal species have dual status in the U.S.

ENDANGERED

Species

BULLETIN

U.S. Department of the Interior
Fish and Wildlife Service
Washington, D.C. 20240

FIRST CLASS
POSTAGE AND FEES PAID
U.S. DEPARTMENT OF THE INTERIOR
PERMIT NO. G-77

REGIONAL NEWS & RECOVERY UPDATES

Volunteers assist in the transplanting and care of Applegate's milk-vetch seedlings at Miller's Island, Oregon.
Photo © Darren Borgias/The Nature Conservancy

Regional endangered species staffers have provided the following news:

Region 1

Applegate's Milk-vetch Staff from the FWS Klamath Falls, Oregon, Office enlisted the Oregon Department of Agriculture (ODA) Plant Conservation Program in planting nearly 900 Applegate's milk-vetch (*Astragalus applegatei*) seedlings. This species is one of Oregon's most endangered plants. Only a handful of populations remain, all located near Klamath Falls. The transplanted seedlings were grown at Oregon State University by ODA staff with FWS funding. The new population is located on Miller Island, a State-owned wildlife management area.

Oil Spill One year to the day after oil spilled from the tanker vessel *Command* off the coast of San Mateo County, California, the U.S. Attorney's Office announced that it had agreed to settlement terms with the parties responsible for the spill. The vessel's owner and the operator agreed to pay approximately $4 million in damages for natural resource injuries, primarily to seabirds, resulting from the incident. The money will be used by a Natural Resource Trustee Council, made up of members from the FWS, National Oceanic and Atmospheric Administration, California Department of Fish and Game, California State Lands Commission, and California Department of Parks and Recreation, to design and implement restoration projects. The settlement funds are expected to

Oregon spotted frog Representatives of the Nisqually National Wildlife Refuge (NWR), Washington Department of Fish and Wildlife, Washington Department of Transportation, Thurston County Conservation District, and The Nature Conservancy met in April 1999 to discuss conservation needs for Oregon spotted frogs (*Rana pretiosa*) in Thurston County, Washington. Potential actions by each party were discussed. A field trip included visits to the main populations at Dempsey Creek and an adjacent site by area wetland mitigation site.

Applegate's milk-vetch in bloom
Photo © Darren Borgias/The Nature Conservancy

be allocated to seabird restoration and additional projects to address shoreline habitat and bird bio-manity. The FWS, represented by our Sacramento Fish and Wildlife Office, participated as the lead Federal trustee agency for the natural resource damage assessment activities. Working with the Department of the Interior Solicitor's Office, we were also instrumental in having an additional $200,000 of settlement funds resulting from Endangered Species Act violations allocated to the Law Enforcement Rewards Fund.

Summer Chum Salmon The Washington State Ecosystems Conservation Program (WSECP) of the U.S. Fish and Wildlife Service's (FWS) Western Washington Office has completed restoration work on a spawning channel at the University of Washington's Big Beef Creek Research Station in Kitsap County. The renovated channel will provide stable spawning habitat and monitoring opportunities for Hood Canal summer chum salmon (*Oncorhynchus keta*), listed as threatened in March 1999. Hood Canal summer chum have been considered extirpated in the Big Beef Creek system since the late 1980's, but the nearby Quilcene National Fish Hatchery has been propagating summer chum, using brood stock from the Quilcene River, and reintroducing them to the system.

FWS employee with chum salmon at Quilcene National Fish Hatchery
Photo by Ron Wong

The WSECP in the Western Washington Office has also completed restoration of 4 acres (1.6 ha) of wetlands and 20 acres (8 ha) of juvenile salmon rearing habitat on the property of West Weber in Snohomish County. The restoration included construction of a series of arms in an abandoned ditch to restore juvenile salmon access to a 16-acre (6.4 ha) wetland. The arms also increase the wetland

ENDANGERED SPECIES BULLETIN NOVEMBER/DECEMBER 1999 VOLUME XXIV NO 6

REGIONAL NEWS & RECOVERY UPDATES

Bald eagle
Coral Gulp photo

acreage by 4 acres. The wetland and a 50-foot (15-meter) buffer on both sides of the ditch will be replanted with a mixture of native conifers and wetland shrubs in spring 2000. Project partners include the landowner, Adopt-a-Stream Foundation, Stilly-Snohomish Fisheries Enhancement Task Force, Stillaguamish Tribe, and Snohomish Conservation District.

Bald Eagle (*Haliaeetus leucocephalus*) FWS staff biologist Doug Laye assisted the fire crew from the Klamath Basin NWR Complex with the first prescribed fires in almost a decade at Bear Valley NWR in Oregon. This refuge was designated specifically for its value as a winter roost for bald eagles and is host to hundreds of bald eagles in the winter and early spring. A total of 40 acres (16 ha) were under-burned in an area that had been thinned by timber operations last year. The thinning was designed specifically to benefit the growth and maintenance of large trees used by the eagles for roosting and nesting.

Reported by LaRee Brosseau of the FWS Portland, Oregon, Regional Office.

Region 5

Endangered Bats The FWS West Virginia Field Office, Canaan Valley NWR, and West Virginia Division of Natural Resources' Non-Game Wildlife and Natural Heritage Program joined to construct a large angle-iron gate at the entrance of Schoolhouse Cave in Pendleton County, West Virginia. The gate, which is designed to protect a large summer colony of the endangered Virginia big-eared bat (*Corynorhinus townsendii virginianus*). A small number of Indiana bats (*Myotis sodalis*) and two species of concern, the Eastern woodrat (*Neotoma floridana*) and the small-footed bat (*Myotis subulatus*), will also be protected by the gate.

Bat gate at Schoolhouse Cave
USFWS photo

The gating project was partially funded by the FWS Chesapeake Bay/Susquehanna River Ecosystem program. Our West Virginia Field Office contracted with Roy Powers of the American Cave Conservation Association to design and direct the construction. Other FWS personnel key to completion of the project came from the Ohio River Islands NWR, FWS Pennsylvania Field Office, and Patuxent NWR. Participants in the project also included The Nature Conservancy, U.S. Forest Service, and National Speleological Society chapters (or Grottoes) from Ohio, Virginia, West Virginia, and Maryland. Forty-six people participated in the effort.

Reported by William A. Tolin, Endangered Species Specialist in the FWS West Virginia Field Office in Elkins.

ON THE WEB

The Fish and Wildlife Service's Endangered Species Homepage provides a wealth of information on our Endangered Species Program:

Listing Web Page
http://endangered.fws.gov/listing
View or download recent listing notices or actions published in the *Federal Register*. Find out which animals and plants are protected by viewing species lists, visit the frequently asked questions to learn more about the listing process, petition management, listing candidates, "candidate conservation agreements with assurances" for private property owners, and critical habitat designations.

Habitat Conservation Planning Web Page
http://endangered.fws.gov/hcp
Go to this website for details on the habitat conservation planning process, download the HCP Handbook, and view a list of HCPs and the species they address.

Recovery Web Page
http://endangered.fws.gov/recovery
An overview of the recovery program and reclassification and delisting activities and more is provided on the recovery program's web page. Recovery plans approved during 1994-1998 are available online at http://endangered.fws.gov/recovery/regions/.

Law Enforcement
http://www.le.fws.gov/
Learn about our nation's wildlife laws and take a virtual tour of the National Fish and Wildlife Forensics Laboratory. Information on wildlife permits is also available.

Listing Actions
http://endangered.fws.gov/frpubs/99frdrlg.html
View or download new listing actions, policies, and other announcements as published in the *Federal Register*.

Prepared by Julia Bumbaca of the FWS Division of Endangered Species, Branch of Information Management, at the Service's Arlington, Virginia, headquarters office.

ENDANGERED SPECIES BULLETIN NOVEMBER/DECEMBER 1999 VOLUME XXIV NO 6

LISTING ACTIONS

During August and September 1999, the Fish and Wildlife Service and National Marine Fisheries Service (NMFS) published the following Endangered Species Act (ESA) listing actions in the *Federal Register*. The full text of each proposed and final rule can be accessed through our website: http://endangered.fws.gov.

Proposed Rules

Aleutian Canada Goose (*Branta canadensis leucopareia*) This unique subspecies nests only on a few of Alaska's remote Aleutian Islands and winters in areas of California and Oregon. It was originally listed as endangered after an introduced predator, the arctic fox, almost eliminated the geese from their nesting grounds. By the mid-1970's, the Aleutian Canada goose population numbered only in the hundreds.

Aleutian Canada goose
Photo by Gale Stuart/USFWS

For the past several decades, biologists have worked intensively to remove the non-native foxes, reintroduce geese back onto the fox-free islands, research migration routes, and protect wintering habitat. Today, we estimate that the Aleutian Canada goose numbers more than 32,000 birds and is no longer in danger of extinction. On August 3, we proposed to recognize the bird's recovery by removing it from the list of threatened and endangered species. (See "A Spectacular Summer for Birds" in *Bulletin* Vol. XXIV, No. 4.)

Golden Sedge (*Carex lutea*) A perennial in the family Cyperaceae, the golden sedge has yellowish green, grass-like leaves and produces stems that may reach 3 feet (0.9 meter) or more with many flowers. This plant is native to the coastal plains of North Carolina, where it is associated with wet pine savannas on sites underlain with calcareous (chalky) deposits. Historically its open habitat was maintained by periodic wildfires.

Scaleshell mussel

Critical Habitat On August 3, we proposed to designate Critical Habitat in parts of Orange and San Diego counties, California, for the tidewater goby (*Eucyclogobius newberryi*), a small endangered fish. Such a designation requires Federal agencies to ensure that any actions they fund, authorize, or carry out are not likely to adversely modify the Critical Habitat. Descriptions and maps of the proposed Critical Habitat areas were published as part of the proposal.

The golden sedge currently is known only from eight populations in Pender and Onslow counties. Most of these populations are small, and some are on privately owned lands vulnerable to draining, development, mining, fire suppression, and a variety of other changes in habitat management. On August 16, we proposed to list this rare plant as endangered. We are also working with the State of North Carolina (which already considers the plant endangered), The Nature Conservancy, and landowners on cooperative protection and management plans.

Scaleshell Mussel (*Leptodea leptodon*) A freshwater mollusk, the scaleshell mussel has a thin, fragile shell that measures up to about 4 inches (10 centimeters) in width and is marked with faint green rays. It once inhabited 53 rivers or streams throughout most of the eastern United States, with populations found as far west as Oklahoma. Like many of the native mussels, however, the scaleshell has declined drastically in range and numbers. Today, populations of this species are known in only 13 rivers in Missouri, Arkansas, and Oklahoma, and we believe 30 of these populations are continuing to decline. Accordingly, on August 13, we proposed to list the scaleshell mussel as endangered.

Threats to the scaleshell, as with many other mussels species, include degraded water quality due to pollution and sedimentation, alteration of habitat through the damming, dredging, or channelizing of waterways, and competition with non-native species like the zebra mussel (*Dreissena polymorpha*). Because the range of the scaleshell overlaps those of several other endangered or threatened mussel species, we do not expect that a decision to list the scaleshell would have any significant additional impacts on river use.

Final Rules

Ten Hawaiian Plants The following plant taxa native to the Maui Nui group of Hawaiian islands (Maui, Molokai, Lanai, and Kaho'olawe) were listed on September 3 as endangered:
- *Clermontia samuelii* or (in Hawaiian) *oha wai*, a shrub in the bellflower family (Campanulaceae);
- *Cyanea copelandii* ssp. *haleakalaensis* or *haha*, a vine-like shrub in the bellflower family;
- *Cyanea glabra* or *haha*, a branched shrub;
- *Cyanea hamatiflora* ssp. *hamatiflora* or *haha*, a palm-like tree;
- *Dubautia plantaginea* ssp. *humilis*, or *na naa e*, a dwarfed shrub in the sunflower family (Asteraceae);
- *Hedyotis schlechtendahliana* var. *remyi* or *kopa*, a subshrub in the coffee family (Rubiaceae);
- *Kanaloa kahoolawensis*, a densely branched shrub in the legume family (Fabaceae);
- *Labordia tinifolia* var. *lanaiensis* or *kamakahala*, an erect shrub or small tree in the logan family (Loganiaceae);
- *Labordia triflora* or *kamakahala*, a climbing plant; and
- *Melicope munroi* or *alani*, a sprawling shrub in the citrus family (Rutaceae).

ENDANGERED SPECIES BULLETIN NOVEMBER/DECEMBER 1999 VOLUME XXIV NO 6

192
...

**GRAPHIC
DESIGNER'S
COLOR
HANDBOOK**

These figures illustrate the imposition of an eight-page layout, with folding dummies, and examples of the front and back of an eight-page signature. The blue and red lines represent folding and trimming lines.

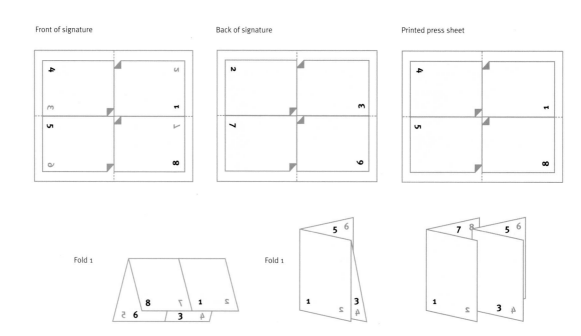

Front of signature

Back of signature

Printed press sheet

Fold 1

Fold 1

The same brochure is illustrated here being printed on a continuous roll of paper on a web press. Large press runs justify the costs of setting up and running this high-speed printing equipment.

Colorful
Words
from the
Pressroom

An imposition-folding dummy shows exactly how this sixteen-page signature will be laid out on press. You can use it to evaluate the positioning of design elements before sending the project to the printer.

Front of signature

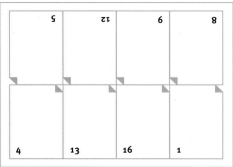

Back of signature

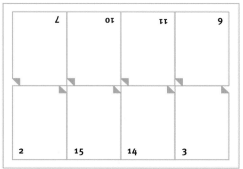

Printed press sheet

First fold

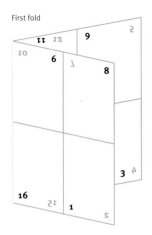

Second fold

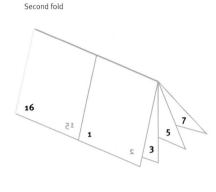

195
...

Colorful
Words
from the
Pressroom

Third fold

Fold 1
Fold 2
Fold 3

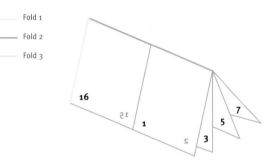

The Sheet Size on Press

PRESS SHEET SIZES AND LAYOUTS can affect the operator's ability to make press adjustments. Control panels allow operators to make incremental ink-flow adjustments about 1 inch apart. These adjustments control ink density from the sheet's leading edge to its trailing edge as it passes through the press. This can be a significant factor in layout, especially when critical color images are positioned one behind the other. Tweaking color densities to improve one image can have detrimental effects on the image that follows it on the sheet.

These figures illustrate the direction of ink adjustments on the press. All adjustments affect the sheet from the leading edge toward the trailing edge, as the arrows show.

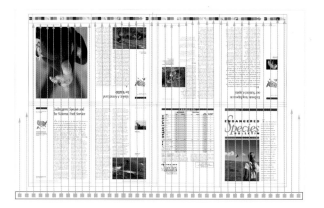

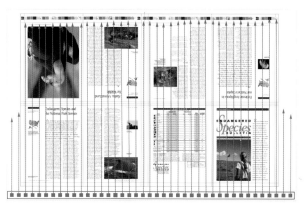

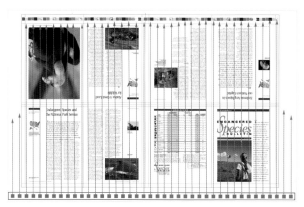

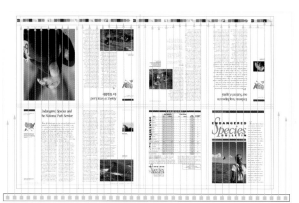

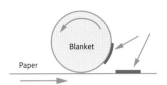

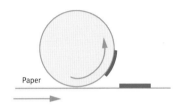

Offset presses, whether sheetfed or web, have the same ink flow characteristics from the lead to trailing edge of the plate. This figure shows a cutaway view of paper traveling through a sheetfed printer.

Colorful
Words
from the
Pressroom

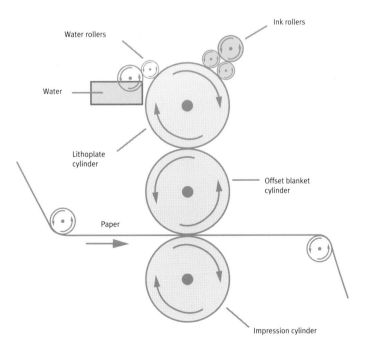

A similar view of the web process shows paper traveling from a continuous roll of paper.

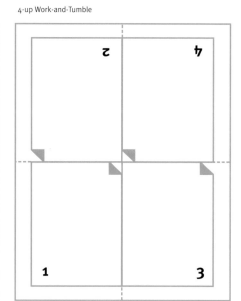

Work and turns are staples of the printing process. Work and tumbles, though less common, are also effective for jobs that don't require precise image placement. In both cases, you print both sides of a press sheet with the same set of plates. In a work and turn, the gripper edge is the same in both passes, enabling precise placement. In a work and tumble, the gripper edge on the first pass becomes the trailing edge on the second.

Work and Turns

ONE OF THE COMMONLY MISUNDER-STOOD concepts in print production work is the *work and turn*. A work and turn job is laid out so that both sides of a job can be printed with one set of plates. The front side of the job is imaged on one half of the plate, with the back side imaged on the other. You can run sheets through the press, and then turn them over and run them again with the same plates, with the images backing up in perfect imposition. An eight-page signature for an 8 ½ x 11-inch publication can be run as a sixteen-page work and turn on a 40-inch press. For very long runs, an 8 ½ x 11-inch brochure can be printed on a 40-inch press as a work and turn, yielding sixteen finished pieces per *sheet*—with one set of plates. Printers who use work and turns effectively can save a great deal of setup and press time, and a lot of money.

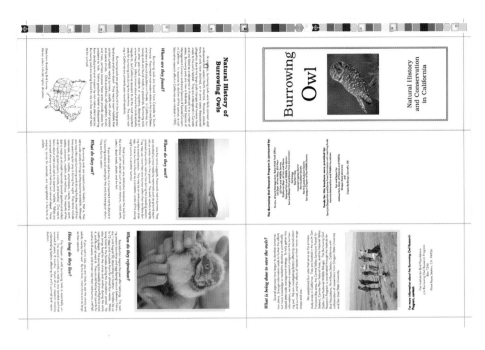

This brochure can be printed effectively as a work and turn on a 12 ½ x 19-inch press sheet.

In this configuration of a work and turn, you're getting twice the value. This is a good option for longer runs and requires only a single set of plates.

Colorful
Words
from the
Pressroom

200
...

**GRAPHIC
DESIGNER'S
COLOR
HANDBOOK**

Excellent color reproduction typically requires high-quality inks, premium-coated papers, and well-adjusted presses. Printing companies that offer these combinations may not offer the lowest prices, but they will give you the highest quality for your dollar.

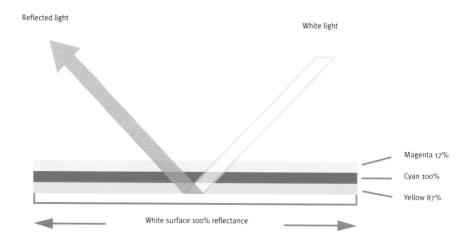

Reflected light

White light

Magenta 17%

Cyan 100%

Yellow 87%

White surface 100% reflectance

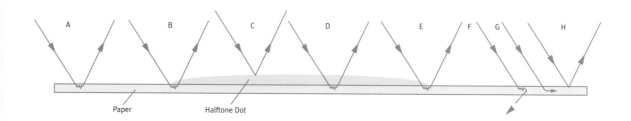

A B C D E F G H

Paper

Halftone Dot

A,B,D,E: diffuse reflection

F: transmission

B,E: Yule-Nielsen effect

C,H: direct reflection

G: absorption by the paper

Light is reflected from—and absorbed by—proofs and printed sheets in a variety of ways. This illustration provides a simplified view of how light sources interact with images as they reflect back to your eyes. The pigments and sub-strates used in proofs are not identical to those used in offset printing, and minor variations are inevitable.

Press Register

MECHANICAL REGISTRATION ON PRESS refers to the precise positioning of the sheet's *lead edge* and *guide side*, which function as reference points to ensure that images print in exactly the same position on every sheet. This is sometimes overlooked on modern multicolor presses because all colors are printed in a single pass. The colors will be in register with each other, but the composite images may bounce around, resulting in slight variations in their position on each sheet. This can play havoc with the bindery process, because folding machines rely on consistent image placement from sheet to sheet to make multiple folds accurately.

201
...

Colorful
Words
from the
Pressroom

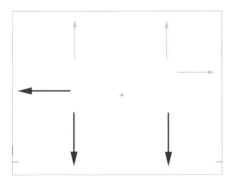
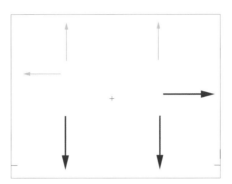

These figures illustrate a press sheet's lead edge and guide side, which provide reference points for precise positioning of images. The gray arrows point to the *wild* sides of the sheet opposite the lead edge and guide side. Minor variations in sheet sizes are inevitable, but as long as the lead edge and guide sides are registering, the wild sides won't influence the final trimming and binding processes.

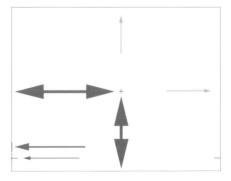

The two double-ended red arrows show the relationship of the lead edge and guide side. The next smaller arrow points to the *side guide* mark on the sheet's edge. The smallest red arrow points to the lead edge register marks. The gray arrows indicate the wild sides.

These figures illustrate the registration check of several successive sheets pulled as the press is running. Fanned out on the press table, they show the registration of the front and back sides of the job. Good press register shows the side guide mark in position on the edge of each sheet, and the lead edge registration marks form a straight line across the sheet edges.

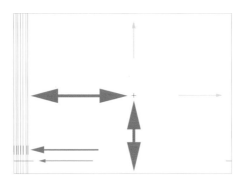

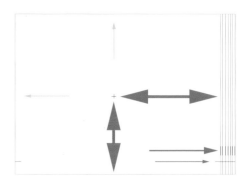

Misregistering guide sides will cause the side guide marks to move into, or completely off of the sheet edge. Again, the result is that the image moves out of position in relationship to the sheet's edge. This can be a common cause of trimming and binding problems that may go unnoticed by the print buyer.

It's a Colorful World

DESIGNERS WILL GIVE YOU A PORT-FOLIO full of reasons why they chose their profession. Whether those reasons are creative, technical, or financial pales in comparison to the ultimate reason— freedom. The design world, whether it's in print or cyberspace, is a vast and complex place where eccentricities and creative liberties allow individuals to flourish personally and professionally. As long as there's color in the world, there will always be designers, artists, and printers who combine their talents to bring those brilliant colors to life.

SUMMARY

COLOR REPRODUCTION IS A HIGHLY technical process that is subject to more variables than any other production industry. Virtually every print project is customized by designers as a unique product, and good understanding of the techniques and variables involved in the process can be used to your best advantage. Excellent quality in this industry is a moving target, and printers who provide consistent results make ongoing investments in maintaining high standards. Always remember that low bid prices may come at a high cost in quality.

Understanding press configurations and layouts can help you refine your designs and can ensure that you get the best possible value for your printing budget. This is the kind of knowledge that will provide you with consistent and beautifully reproduced designs, job after job.

204
...

GRAPHIC
DESIGNER'S
COLOR
HANDBOOK

COLOR ON THE WEB

The CMYK process reigns
supreme in print media. But on
the World Wide Web, RGB is
king, with colors composed
from combinations of red,
green, and blue.

When red, green, and blue are combined at full intensity, the monitor displays white, as shown in this screen shot. You can verify this on your own monitor with a 10x magnifying glass or loupe.

Seeing Red, Green, and Blue

FOR MOST OF THIS BOOK, we've concentrated on the use of color in print production. But the discussion wouldn't be complete without exploring the options available to designers targeting the World Wide Web.

Designing for the Web requires instinct, luck, and retraining your discerning eye. In the world of CMYK print production, a designer who errantly submits an RGB file will suffer repercussions. By contrast, the Web embraces RGB.

As noted in Chapter 3, the RGB color model is additive. When you combine red, green, and blue at their full intensity, you see white on the monitor. When RGB intensity is zero, you see black. By combining RGB in various percentages, you can generate the 16.7 million colors available on a 24-bit display.

206
...

GRAPHIC
DESIGNER'S
COLOR
HANDBOOK

The simplified cutaway view of a computer monitor shows the electron gun firing at full intensity through a single color pixel. The figure on the facing page illustrates a surface printed in CMYK, which depends on the reflection of ambient light.

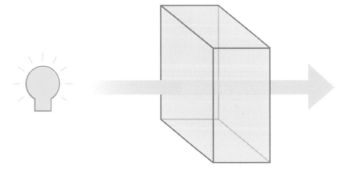

Specifying Color for the Web

SAVVY WEB DESIGNERS are well versed in RGB, but for novices, it helps to begin from scratch and learn how these colors are created. RGB colors are specified by numeric values between 0 and 255 that determine the intensity of red, green, and blue. Higher numbers equal greater intensity. For example, values of 255 red, 255 green, and 255 blue generate white. Values of 0 red, 0 green, and 0 blue generate black. Values of 0 red, 0 green, and 255 blue generate a pure RGB blue.

In theory, an RGB monitor can show up to 16.7 million colors. But in practice, this number is limited by several factors, most importantly the file format you're using and the maximum *bit depth* of your computer display.

Each pixel you see on a computer screen is described internally as a series of zeroes and ones, the bits—short for binary digits—that represent the fundamental building blocks of all computer data. The number of bits used to describe each pixel determines how many colors the computer can display. For example, in an 8-bit image, each pixel is defined by a combination of eight zeroes or ones. The image is thus limited to 256 colors, because there are only 256 possible combinations of bits: 00000000, 00000001, 00000010, 00000011, and so on, up to 11111111. A 24-bit image uses 24 zeroes or ones to describe each pixel, and can thus display up to 16.7 million (256 x 256 x 256) colors. A 16-bit image can show up to 65,536 (256 x 256) colors.

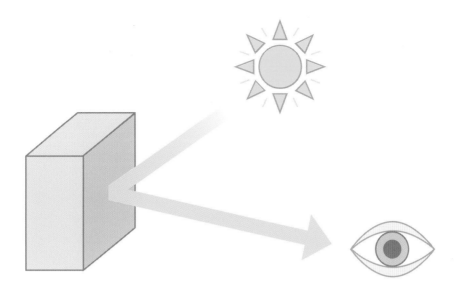

Thus, if you specify color values of 133 red, 96 green, and 168 blue, the computer translates them internally into their binary equivalents: 10000101 for red, 01100000 for green, and 10101000 for blue. The result is a light violet—as long as you have a 24-bit monitor. Although 24-bit displays are increasingly common, many older computer systems are limited to eight or 16 bits (this is actually a limitation of the graphics adapter that drives the display—almost all color monitors are 24-bit capable). If you try to display a 24-bit image on one of these computers, the system uses a technique known as *color reduction* to translate any colors it can't show into their nearest neighbors from the smaller system palette. In many images, especially photos, this color reduction causes banding in areas that should have smooth color gradations.

It's important to keep these points in mind when you're preparing Web graphics, because you generally want your designs to be viewable on the widest possible range of computers.

Additionally, the popular Graphics Interchange Format (GIF)—commonly used to produce stylized type treatments, line art, animated banner ads, and other design elements that require sharp detail—is limited to a maximum of 8 bits, or 256 colors. To reduce the size of these files, experienced Web designers often use software-based color-reduction techniques to further limit the color palette. Leading image-editing programs, such as Adobe Photoshop and Macromedia Fireworks, include features that let you see the effects of GIF color reduction, so you can achieve an optimal balance between image quality and file size. Effectively

making such trade-offs is a major challenge of Web design. For example, it's often wise to apply *antialiasing* when you're creating type treatments that will be saved as GIF files. Antialiasing smoothes jagged edges in type and line art by slightly blurring pixels along the edges, but it also increases the number of colors.

The Joint Photographic Experts Group (JPEG) format, generally used to reproduce photographs and fine art, employs the full 24-bit RGB palette. Here, you reduce file sizes by applying greater or lesser levels of compression. A high degree of compression tends to reduce the image's sharpness, but has little or no effect on the range of colors.

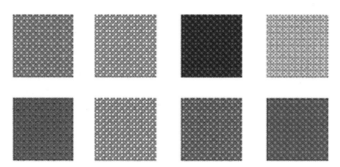

Venturing outside the original Web-safe color palette can create unsightly dithering patterns when images are viewed on 8-bit displays. These blocks illustrate the effect of dithering on different colors.

208
...

GRAPHIC
DESIGNER'S
COLOR
HANDBOOK

The Web-Safe Palette

WEB DESIGNERS ARE ACCUSTOMED to working with the 216 colors that comprise the *Web-safe palette*. Colors in this palette can be shown on any Mac or PC monitor, even if it's limited to a maximum of 256 colors. The number of colors is less than 256 due to differences between the Mac and Windows system palettes.

If you specify a color outside the Web-safe palette, it will likely be *dithered* when seen on an 8-bit monitor. Much like a printed halftone, dithering simulates colors that cannot otherwise be displayed by arranging some of the 256 available colors into patterns. Unfortunately, whereas color halftones do a reasonably good job of simulating real-world colors, dithering often produces unsightly arrangements of pixels.

It's important to remember that dithering appears only when you view colors on an 8-bit monitor; almost all computer systems sold these days sport 16- or 24-bit displays. But if you want to ensure that your designs are viewable without dithering on the widest range of computers, you should stick with the 216 Web-safe colors. Many graphics programs include a built-in Web-safe palette as an option. You can either specify Web-safe colors as you're creating a design, or use color-reduction tools to convert existing designs into a Web-safe format.

This palette applies primarily when you're creating GIF files, or specifying color elements within an HTML-authoring program, such as Adobe GoLive or Macromedia Dreamweaver. JPEG images, as we noted above, use a full 24-bit color palette that can't be reduced.

Testing for Variation

VARIATIONS AMONG BROWSERS, displays, and operating systems make it virtually impossible to ensure the absolute accuracy of colors on the Web. In addition to considering different display capabilities, designers need to account for differences in the way Macintosh and Windows systems show color. By default, images displayed on Windows systems are slightly darker than those displayed on the Mac. Additionally, Microsoft's Internet Explorer and Netscape Navigator have subtle variations in the way they render graphics. It's thus important to test your Web designs as they'll be seen on a variety of monitors, platforms, and browsers. You can simulate these variations to some degree by setting your display to a lower bit-depth, or by adjusting the monitor brightness. For example, the Macintosh operating system includes a monitor-calibration utility that lets you reset the display *gamma*—a technical term for overall brightness and contrast—to match that of a Windows PC.

Extensive testing improves the odds that your creation will be displayed with predictable results on the system your client is using—and just as importantly, on the systems *their* clients are using.

Color is tricky business on the Web. Warm and cool colors can be vibrant on some systems and muted on others. These variations can be difficult to track, as most designers don't have all platforms on their desks. You're best bet is to stick with Web-safe colors until you're comfortable creating new customized palettes, especially on crucial color-dependent projects.

RGB images, as you can see from this photo, will vary from one computer system or browser to another. In this case, the differences are noticeable, but don't detract from the quality of the image.

Effective Web Presentations

THE WEB PRESENTS A NEW SET OF challenges for designers accustomed to working in print. For example, the feel of a printed piece often has a direct effect on how it's perceived. The Web, in contrast, is a more purely visual medium, while adding a degree of interaction that isn't possible in print. Due to the fundamental differences between the CMYK and RGB color models, many colors, such as pastels, muted hues, and neutral shades, change drastically when transferred to the Web. It can't be overstated that learning the Web color process requires practice and some diligent research.

Despite the many differences between print and Web design, it's important to stick to your color roots, as most of the same rules apply. Even if you're using the Web-safe palette, you can choose from plenty of warm, cool, and rich colors, as well as a few muted ones. Depending on your project and audience, you still want to assess appearance and marketability as you would for any print job.

Keep It Simple

USER-FRIENDLINESS AND CLARITY are crucial to effective color communication on the Web. While black-and-white copy offers the greatest contrast and easiest readability on a monitor, it's not very appealing to the average Web surfer. You may have a limited number of colors to work with, but it doesn't mean that you have to abandon your classy or flashy designs. Web designs can use any number of visually exciting color combinations that offer easy readability.

Color is particularly important in regard to navigation. If navigation bars and icons are logically placed and/or highlighted with color, navigating the Web page can be effortless. However, nothing will frustrate a viewer as much as running the cursor over an item that appears to be a navigation tool, only to find out that it's simply highlighted text.

The example here provides a good example of a clean site that's easy to read and navigate. Above all, it doesn't sacrifice anything in terms of color usage.

Clean design, effective use of
complementary colors, and
simple navigation tools help
make these user-friendly
Web sites. The logos are easily
visible and navigation buttons
are colorful and interesting.
(Courtesy Paul Baker Printing,
Inc. and Peter King and
Company, Inc.)

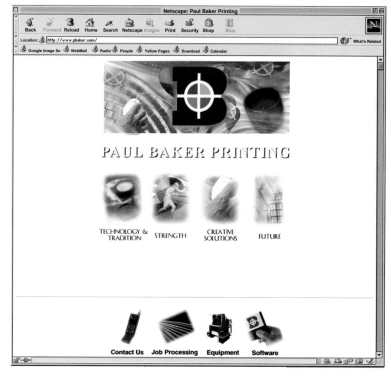

Simplicity in color and style creates harmony on these pages. The logo appears throughout the site without being overbearing, navigation photos are easily recognizable, and concise text makes it very readable. (Courtesy Paul Baker Printing, Inc.)

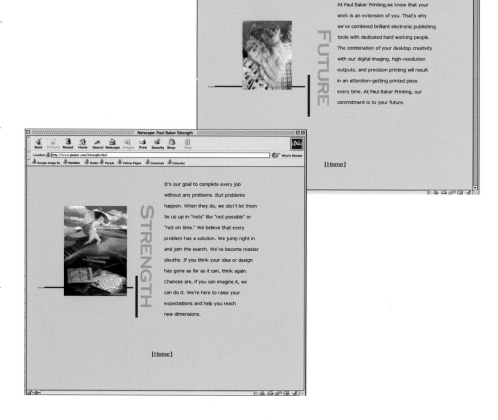

Both of these pages make a powerful statement by using a strong background color that complements the bold images. The design and coordinating colors are simple and elegant. (Courtesy Paul Baker Printing, Inc.)

Because of the freedom the Web affords, it's easy to throw caution to the wind, overdesign your elements, and splash too much color onto a Web page. Cramming too much information and using a wild variety of colors can cause a cluttered look that many will find confusing and frustrating. These sites can trigger disconcerting color responses.

Think about sites you've visited and make mental notes of what you've seen. We've all surfed obnoxious sites flooded with blinding backgrounds, Day-Glo fonts, and animated critters doing the samba, but can you recall what the site was about? If there's a lesson, it's that nothing is wrong with keeping things simple.

Scanning for the Web

THE EXPENSE OF BUILDING AND maintaining Web pages often justifies the use of professionally scanned images. While you may consider an inexpensive desktop scanner to be "good enough," the difference in the final page will be noticeable. Because images on the Web are 72 dpi, your prepress house can *scan to disk* for nominal fees. These scans are usually provided without hard proofs, which most designers find unnecessary if the scans are from a good source. Once you have the disk, you can *soft proof* the images by viewing and adjusting them on your monitor. If you are producing images simultaneously for print and Web, your prepress house can scan at a higher resolution suitable for CMYK production and then down-sample the images to a lower resolution for use on the Web.

Overuse of bright colors can have your audience literally seeing spots. If you stare at the center of the green square for thirty seconds without wavering, and then quickly shift your view to the center of the white square, you'll see red.

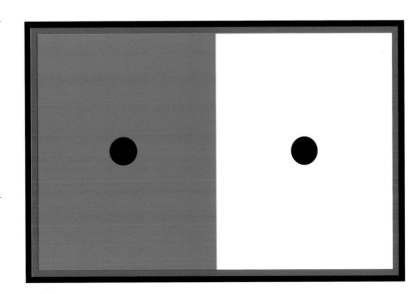

214
...

**GRAPHIC
DESIGNER'S
COLOR
HANDBOOK**

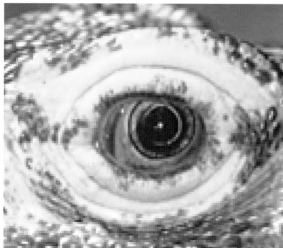

Images scanned at 72 dpi are generally unsuitable for traditional CMYK reproduction but look fine on the Web.

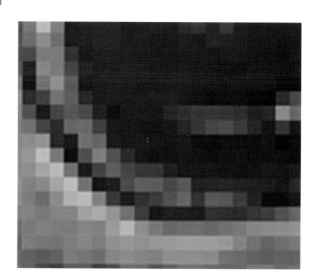

Color and Contrast

TEXT PLACED OVER COLOR elements provides good contrast and can be highly readable. Remember that about one out of twelve males has some degree of color blindness. If you've used sufficient contrast between background and text, most of your audience will receive your message without difficulty, even if the colors are a little skewed for their individual visual interpretations.

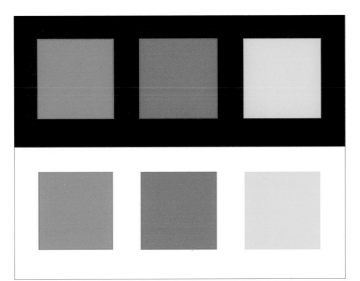

The phenomenon known as simultaneous contrast can create optical illusions. In this illustration, colors within the black box appear to be larger and lighter than the same color blocks duplicated below.

Good contrast results in a pleasing and readable appearance. Too little contrast can make the text virtually unreadable. Too much contrast in complementary colors can make them visually jarring.

CONTRAST
CONTRAST
CONTRAST
CONTRAST
CONTRAST
CONTRAST
CONTRAST
CONTRAST
CONTRAST

CONTRAST
CONTRAST
CONTRAST
CONTRAST
CONTRAST
CONTRAST
CONTRAST
CONTRAST
CONTRAST

Thematic Use of Color

BEYOND THE USE OF A WEB-SAFE or custom palette, you can establish harmonious color themes by sampling colors from photographs or other images on a Web page.

Each of the following images expresses a different theme, and each can be used as a sample for planning a color scheme. Many designers have made this a permanent part of their color regime, and do so automatically when a new job lands on the desk. The frames that surround each image often set the tone of the color scheme, whether it's warm, cool, rich, muted, elegant, or playful. The accompanying color blocks are sampled from the photo. The more you experiment with various frames and blocks, the more surprised you'll be at which colors ultimately serve the your purpose. Over time, you'll develop an eye for which colors work best, and you'll be able to create a secure and stable Web-color repertoire.

216
...

GRAPHIC
DESIGNER'S
COLOR
HANDBOOK

Warm colors

The red frame in this sample, along with the accompanying swatches, exudes warmth. Cool colors can provide contrast to these images but should be used sparingly. Warm colors are comfortable and passionate and usually add appeal to anything they surround. Even the dark chocolate colors provide depth and richness.

Neutrals

Neutrals, muted colors, and earthtones can be challenging to replicate on the Web. In this case, running a sample is advisable. The neutral colors shown here mix and match well with most designs, and provide a calming effect.

Vibrant colors

Vibrant blues, reds, greens, yellows, and pinks work well in contrast with calmer colors but also combine well with each other. This parrot shows how a palette full of screaming color can bring balance, boldness, and fun to a design.

Metallics

Metallics are as difficult to match as glassware, but you can always fall back on an elegant color scheme. In addition to the gray and silver hues, you'll easily find success in deep, rich burgundy, purple, royal blue, and hunter green. For contrast, yellow, white, and lighter pastels will punch out of the darker tones without interrupting the feel of your design.

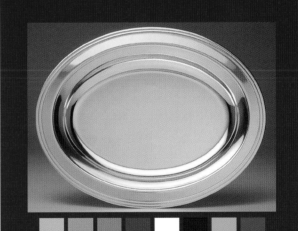

Food images

Designs involving food or other consumer products can be tricky but certainly not impossible. If you have a strong image, such as this sandwich, it's best to let the ingredients speak for themselves. The strong frame is matched to the olives and sets the tone for the scheme. The yellow, green, white, red, and brown are all vibrant, so to avoid overwhelming the viewer, you should use them sparingly.

218
...

GRAPHIC
DESIGNER'S
COLOR
HANDBOOK

Cool Colors

The deep blue hues coupled with bright yellow add to the chill of this image. This is a case where cooler is better. Adding reds, oranges, or magentas would spoil the rugged appeal.

Glass Images

Designs involving glassware are always a challenge, and many designers are frustrated by the lack of available color. But take another look—reflections and accessories offer color depth that can be drawn into the body of a design. In this case, the last color you would think to match, lime green, affords the best flexibility. Images with rough textured backgrounds also offer a range of colors, as seen in this photo.

Busy Images

Designers often find themselves frustrated with busy images that contain too much color. For these designs, swatches are paramount. Here, the yellow frame helps center and lighten the image without washing out the metallic golds. What may seem a daunting task is made easier when you pull the lesser colors into the swatches. Any of the red, blues, or browns could easily be used as highlight colors. But remember, with a busy image, a little goes a long way.

Bold Colored Objects

Images with bold colored elements and muted backgrounds can be deceptively difficult to sample for color themes. The red and yellow are eye-catching, but they fail as dominant colors. The surrounding green and brownstone cause the image to fall flat. Your best bet is to search for a small highlight color to pull the scheme together. In this case, the blue from her skirt was the best option.

Minimal Color Schemes

This image is a perfect example of how to build a color scheme around shades and hues of only two colors. The deep teals and purples add to the mystery and aura of the image. Modern or abstract designs can generally handle all types of color schemes, from bold to subtle.

Subjects with Contrast

Images that contain many contrasting and colored elements are difficult under any circumstances. In this image, setting up a color scheme is made infinitely more challenging by the falling water, bright green/yellow turf, and red shadows cast by the umbrella. When none of the colors in an image match in combination, the best approach is to use a darker shade of the most offending color. The brightness of the turf matched with a dark green helps contain the other colors, making the image easier to work with.

GLOSSARY

220
...

GRAPHIC
DESIGNER'S
COLOR
HANDBOOK

A

Accordion fold: Two or more parallel folds in which each fold opens in the opposite direction from the previous one, so that the paper opens like an accordion.

Acid-free paper: Paper that contains no acid or acid-producing chemicals.

Additive color: Color produced by combining red, green, and blue light in varying intensities. Computer monitors use additive color, whereas the printing process uses subtractive color.

Against the grain: Folding or printing performed at right angles to the grain direction of the paper.

Antialiasing: A technique that smoothes jagged edges in text and line art on a computer screen by slightly blurring pixels in edge areas.

Antioffset spray: A dry vegetable starch powder used to help prevent wet ink from transferring from one sheet of paper to another.

Aqueous coating: A water-based paper coating designed to overprint, protect, and enhance printed images.

Artifact: A visible defect in a digital image, often caused by hardware or software limitations.

Automatic image replacement: A process in which low-resolution FPO (for position only) images are automatically replaced by high-resolution images before the final pages are produced.

B

Banding: An undesirable graphic effect in which a gradation contains visible stepping of shades.

Basis weight: The weight in pounds of a ream (five hundred sheets) of paper, cut to a standard size according to the grade of paper.

Bindery: The department within a printing plant that handles binding and trimming. Some companies operate as specialized binderies for printers.

Binding: The fastening of assembled sheets or signatures along one edge of a publication. The binding process also includes folding, gathering, trimming, stitching, gluing, and other finishing steps.

Bit: Short for "binary digit," the fundamental building block of all computer data. A bit can be either a zero or a one.

Bit depth: The number of bits that can be captured by a scanner or shown on a display. An 8-bit image is limited to 256 colors; a 24-bit image can show up to 16.7 million colors.

Bit map: A digital image composed of dots.

Black plate: Also referred to as the *black printer*, this printing plate is used along with cyan, magenta, and yellow plates in four-color (CMYK) process printing. Also called the key plate, its purpose is to enrich the contrast of the final reproduction.

Black and white: Originals or reproductions in which black is the only color.

Blanket: A rubber material that is clamped around the cylinder on a printing press, to which the image is transferred from the printing plate, and from which the image is transferred to the paper.

Bleed: The portion of an image that extends beyond the trim area of a page.

Bleed allowance: The degree to which a bleed must extend beyond a document's trim to allow for variations in cutting and folding.

Blend: An area in an image that transitions from one color (or gray level) to another. Also known as a graduated tint, graduation, or vignette.

Blind image: An image on a printing plate that has lost its ability to hold ink and fails to print.

Blueline: An imposition proof made from stripped film negatives or positives that is used to check the position of page elements before printing.

Body: The viscosity or consistency of an ink.

Bond paper: A grade of paper that often has cotton content and is used for letterheads.

Book paper: A grade of coated or uncoated paper generally used in books and other publications.

Bounce: An undesirable mechanical press registration resulting from the lead edge of the sheet bouncing away from the press head stops.

Break for color: To separate the elements of a design to be printed in different colors.

Brightness: The reflective quality or brilliance of a piece of paper. In color, the amount of light reflected by a particular color.

Brochure: A pamphlet of two or more pages that is folded or bound.

Bump: Ink applied from a fifth plate in four-color process printing to strengthen a specific color. Also referred to as a touch plate.

Burn: To expose light-sensitive emulsions on proofs or plates in a vacuum frame with high-intensity light.

C

C1S: Coated one side. Paper that has a clay coating on only one side, often used for book covers.

C2S: Coated two sides. Paper that has a clay coating on both sides.

Calendaring: A polishing process in which paper passes between calendar rolls to increase its smoothness.

Calendar rolls: Horizontal rolls at the end of a paper machine that polish and smooth the surface of paper as it passes through.

Calibration: The process by which scanners, monitors, printers, and other digital imaging devices are adjusted to more accurately reproduce color.

Caliper: The thickness of paper, plates, or packing material, usually expressed in mils (thousands of an inch).

Cast coated: A paper that has been clay coated and dried under pressure to give it a high-gloss finish.

Chalking: A printing defect, caused by improper drying of ink, in which pigment chalks off, often because the ink vehicle has been absorbed too rapidly into the paper.

Choke: A trapping technique in which one color area is made slightly smaller to allow for misregistration on press. It is used in conjunction with a *spread*, in which another color area is made slightly larger.

CMYK: Cyan, magenta, yellow, black. The colors of the subtractive color system, also known as process colors.

Coated paper: Paper with a smooth clay-coated surface.

Coating: An emulsion, varnish, or lacquer applied to a printed surface to give it added protection or to produce a dramatic special effect.

Color control strip: A series of color bars printed on press sheets designed to help press operators monitor and detect problems with color balance, registration, dot gain, and other printing-related factors.

Color correction: The process by which color values in images are adjusted to correct or compensate for errors in photography, scanning, or separation.

Color Key: An analog proofing system that uses pigmented acetate overlays to represent four-color images.

Color proof: A full-color reproduction of a design made photomechanically or digitally.

Color reduction: The process by which the number of colors in a digital image is reduced so it can be saved at a smaller file size or displayed on an 8-bit monitor.

Color separation: The process of separating artwork into component electronic files or films of cyan, magenta, yellow, and black in preparation for printing.

Commercial printer: A printing company that focuses primarily on print runs of five thousand or more using half-size and full-size printing equipment.

Composition: The process of setting type and arranging elements in a design.

Continuous tone: An image, such as a photograph, in which each dot or particle is composed from a mixture of RGB or CMYK colorants.

Contract proof: The final proof provided by the printer and on which the client signs off, implying that the proof represents the press run, and that the job is ready to print.

Cotton paper: Paper made from cotton fibers rather than, or in addition to, wood fibers.

Cover stock: A variety of heavier papers used for the covers of catalogs, brochures, booklets, and similar publications.

Cromalin: A four-color proof produced with dyes.

Curl: The distortion of a sheet of paper due to absorption of moisture or differences in coating from one side to another.

Cyan: One of the subtractive primary colors used as part of the four-color process inks (cyan, magenta, yellow, and black).

D

Densitometer: An instrument that measures optical density of colors, dot gain, and other printing elements, used to monitor and control consistency throughout a press run.

222
...

GRAPHIC
DESIGNER'S
COLOR
HANDBOOK

Die cut: A letterpress technique that uses sharp steel rules to make cuts in printed sheets.

Distributing rollers: Rubber-covered rollers that transfer ink from the ink fountain and into the ink train of a printing press.

Dot: A single element of a screen lined image.

Dot gain: An inevitable effect of the offset printing process in which dots print larger than desired.

DPI: Dots per inch. The measure of an input or output device's resolution.

Drier: A substance added to ink to make it dry more quickly.

Dryback: The tendency of an ink to dull and lighten as it dries and is absorbed into the paper.

Dull finish: A flat clay coating applied to paper that is duller that gloss coating, and slightly smoother than a matte coating.

Dummy: A preliminary layout showing the size, shape, form, and general style of a printed piece, including folds.

Duotone: A two-color halftone reproduction from a black-and-white or color photograph.

E

Emulsion: A light-sensitive coating on one side of photographic film, proofing materials, or printing plates that faces a light source during exposure.

EPS: Encapsulated PostScript. A popular graphics file format based on Adobe Systems' PostScript technology.

Exposure: The process of producing an image on a light-sensitive, emulsion-coated material, such as film, proofs, or plates.

F

Feeder: The section of a sheet-fed printing press that separates the sheets and feeds them in position for printing.

Fillers: White pigments such as clay, titanium dioxide, and calcium carbonate that are added to paper to improve its opacity, brightness, and printing surface.

Filling in: A condition on a printing press in which the ink fills the area between halftone dots.

Finish: The surface characteristics of paper.

Flier: A one-page, unfolded printed promotional piece.

Fold mark: Horizontal or vertical lines printed outside of the final image area on a sheet of paper to indicate where it should be folded.

Form rollers: The inking or dampening rollers that directly contact the plate on a printing press.

Fountain roller: The rollers in offset lithography that feed ink or water to the inking or dampening roller systems.

Fountain solution: A mixture of water, gum arabic, and other chemicals used to dampen the plate and keep nonprinting areas from accepting ink.

Four-up: The imposition of four items to be printed on the same sheet of paper.

FPO: For position only. A low-resolution or simulated version of a graphic that is used as a placeholder in initial proofing and layout stages.

G

Gamma: A measure of brightness and contrast in photographic images.

Gang: The random combination of several images on a proof. Also, the combination of unrelated jobs on one press sheet.

Gang run: A print run in which two or more print jobs are combined.

Gathering: The process of assembling folded signatures in proper sequence in preparation for binding.

GIF: Graphics Interchange Format. A popular graphics file format primarily used to produce banner ads, type treatments, and line art on the World Wide Web. GIF images are limited to a maximum of 256 colors.

Gloss: The shiny appearance of coated papers or final finish of printed pieces.

Grain: The direction in which the fibers run in a piece of paper.

Gradation: A smooth transition of shades between black and white, between one color and another, or between one color and white. Also called a gradient.

Gripper: A set of pincers that holds and transfers paper through the printing press.

Gripper edge: The leading edge of paper as it passes through a printing press.

Gripper margin: The unprintable edge on which the paper is gripped as it passes through a printing press.

Gutter: The inner margins of two facing pages in a publication.

H

Hairline register: To register color separations within ½ (0.5) point.

Halation: An undesirable blurred effect in photographs, proofs, printing plates, and printed pieces that resembles a halo, usually occurring in highlighted areas or around bright objects, caused by dust particles or improper contact.

Halftone: An image composed from dots of varying sizes that simulate continuous tones.

Hard dot: A dot in photographic images, proofs, and printed pieces that has no noticeable halation around its edges.

Hard proof: A tangible proof, such as laser paper, film, or any of various proofing mediums.

Hexachrome: A trademarked term for a six-color printing process developed by Pantone, Inc.

Hickey: A spot or imperfection in a printed piece due to foreign particles becoming adhered to the printing plates.

Highlights: The lightest tones in an image, represented by the smallest dots in a halftone.

Hue: The attribute of a color that distinguishes it from other colors.

I

Image area: The viable area of a press sheet that can be printed, surrounded by non-image areas, or margins.

Image assembly: The process of stripping film negatives in position prior to proofing and platemaking.

Image editing: The process of modifying photographs and other images, usually performed electronically using software applications.

Imagesetter: A device designed to reproduce graphics and type at high resolution onto film, proofs, or printing plates. Also referred to as an *image recorder*.

Impose: To arrange and position pages for a predetermined press sheet size to meet press, folding, and bindery requirements.

Imposition: A layout of pages positioned for a predetermined press sheet size to meet press, folding, and bindery requirements.

Impression: A printed image applied by pressure from the printing plates, blanket and impression cylinders, as the paper is printed.

Impression cylinder: The cylinder on a printing press that comes in contact with the press sheet and presses the sheet against the image-carrying blanket.

Ink holdout: The appearance and degree to which paper resists ink penetration.

Inkometer: A device that measures the tack, or cohesion, of printing inks.

Ink trap: The capacity for one ink color to print over another ink color smoothly.

Insert: A printed piece that is not part of the original publication but is bound into a magazine, newspaper, or other printed piece.

J

JPEG: (Joint Photographic Experts Group). A popular graphics file format often used to reproduce photographs or fine art on the World Wide Web.

K

Key: A color-coded legend that explains symbols or identifies colors to be printed in a piece of artwork.

Keyline: Artwork for offset reproduction that shows outlines indicating the exact shape, position, and size of halftone elements, line illustrations, and text.

Knockout: To remove the background color on which type or graphics are being printed.

L

Laid paper: Paper in which the surface finish shows a visible pattern of parallel lines.

Laminate: The process of applying a plastic film to a printed piece for protection or appearance.

Laminate proofs: Proofing systems that consist of several layers of pigmented proofing materials adhered in sequence to a substrate.

Lamination: A plastic film applied to a printed piece for protection or appearance.

Letterpress: Printing and die-cutting equipment in which the image to be printed or cut is raised from the plate and applied directly to paper.

Lightfastness: The ability of paper to resist fading or yellowing when exposed to light.

Light table: A table made for assembling film negatives, featuring a translucent top with a light source underneath.

Linen finish: Paper in which the fibers form a linen, or woven finish.

LPI: Lines per inch. The number of rows of halftone cells per inch, also referred to as screen frequency.

M

Machine coated: Paper that is coated on one or both sides on a paper machine.

Magenta: One of the subtractive primary colors (cyan, magenta, yellow, and black) used for four-color process inks.

Makeready: The process of preparing the press for printing a particular job, such as putting ink in the fountains and adjusting registration and ink density before beginning the press run.

Matchprint: A popular contract proofing system.

Matte: A dull, clear coating applied to printed materials for protection or appearance.

Matte finish: A clay coating on paper that is dull, without gloss or luster.

Mechanical: Camera-ready artwork that includes text, photos, illustrations, and so forth. A mechanical can be in the form of an artboard, a digital printout, or a digital file ready for high-resolution output.

Midtones: The tonal range between highlights and shadows in a photograph, proof, or printed piece.

Mock-up: A visual presentation of a design or page layout that approximates what the final printed piece will look like.

Moiré: An undesirable screen pattern caused by incorrect screen angles or rescreening printed images.

Monochrome: A one-color image or page.

Mottle: An undesirable printing effect in which solid areas appear spotty and uneven.

O

Offset printing: One of the most common forms of printing in which images are transferred from an exposed printing plate to a smooth rubber blanket surface and then onto the press sheet.

One-up: To impose only one finished piece on a press sheet.

Opacity: The property of paper or other substrate that minimizes show-through, or image visibility from the back side of the substrate.

Out of register: A print-production error in which the color separations for an image are not properly aligned.

Overprint: To print over an area that has already been printed.

Overrun: The number of printed copies that exceeds the specified print run.

P

Packing: Sheets of calibrated material that are placed between printing plates, blankets, and cylinders to provide proper printing pressure.

Page layout: The assembly of elements on a page, including text and graphics. Also called page composition.

Page proof: A layout of pages as they will appear in the publication or printed piece.

Pagination: The process of arranging the pages of a publication in proper sequence.

Pantone Matching System: A system of inks, color specifications, and color guides for reproducing spot colors.

Paper stock: The paper used for printing a particular project.

PE: Printer's Error. A mistake made by the printer after the client has submitted originals.

Perfect bound: A method of binding in which signatures are folded and collated on top of one another and held together by adhesive.

Perfecting press: A printing press that images both sides of the paper in one pass.

Perforate: To cut or provide cut marks on a printed sheet.

Picking: Paper or ink particles on previously printed press sheets that adhere to blanket or impression cylinders.

PICT: A graphics file format developed by Apple Computer for use on the Macintosh.

Pigment: The solid particles in ink or proofing materials that act as colorants.

Pixel: Short for "picture element," a single dot in an on-screen image.

Plate: Aluminum composite sheets with emulsion coatings that transfer inked images to the blankets.

Plate cylinder: The cylinder of a printing press on which the plate is mounted.

Platemaking: The process of exposing and developing printing plates for press runs.

Positive: Film in which the black and clear areas are the same as the original, as opposed to a film negative.

PostScript: A printing technology developed by Adobe Systems that permits high-quality output of digital images. Adobe licenses the technology to manufacturers of printers, imagesetters, and other output devices.

Prepress: The process of preparing all output elements for printing. The equipment used for mass reproduction of printed materials.

Press check: The examination of press sheets during the makeready process to determine that all elements and colors are correct and in register.

Press proof: A final color proof made on a printing press to verify color and printing quality.

Press run: The act of operating a printing press for a particular project. Also refers to the total number of copies to be printed.

Press sheet: A single printed sample pulled at random during or after a press run.

Print run: The total number of copies to be printed. Also called a press run.

Printer's spread: The imposition of pages as they will be assembled and reproduced on press.

Process color: Four-color reproduction of the full range of colors by the use of four printing plates, one for each of the primary colors: cyan (process blue), magenta (process red), yellow (process yellow), and black (process black).

Progressive proof: Press proofs made from each separate printing plate, showing the sequence of printing as well as the result after each color plate is added to the image.

Proof: A predictable representation of what the printed job should look like.

R

Rasterization: The process of converting a digital image into a series of dots.

Reader's spread: A layout for a printing project that shows pages in the sequence in which they will be read.

Ream: Five hundred sheets of paper.

Reflective art: Artwork that must be photographed by light reflected from its surface.

Register: The fitting of two or more images on the same paper in exact alignment with each other.

Registration mark: Crosshairs or other graphic elements applied to originals, proofs, and printing plates to establish proper image alignment.

Reprint: To print a project again using the original materials.

Resolution: The degree of precision by which images are captured, displayed, or printed. Resolution is generally measured in either dots per inch or the total number of vertical and horizontal pixels.

Retouch: To alter a photograph or illustration, either manually or digitally.

Reverse: To print an image or text in the opposite of the background color, such as white type on a black background.

RGB: Red, green, blue. The colors of the additive color system.

Right-angle fold: Two or more folds that are at right angles to each other.

RIP: Raster Image Processor. A device that converts digital images into a bit-mapped format that can be produced on an imagesetter or other output device.

Roll-fed press: A web-fed press that uses rolls of paper.

Rosette: The flower like pattern created when the four CMYK color halftone screens are printed in register at the traditional angles.

S

Saddle stitched: A form of binding that uses staple-shaped wires through the gutter fold; also called saddle-wired.

Saturation: A measure of the purity of a color, determined by the amount of gray it contains. The higher the gray level, the lower the saturation.

Scale: To reduce or enlarge an image or a page proportionally.

Scanner: A device that captures images on paper or transparencies and converts them into digital information.

Screen frequency: The number of lines per inch (LPI) or dots per inch (DPI) in a halftone screen.

Score: An indented line, usually performed as a letterpress operation, on a sheet of paper that makes it easier to fold.

Screen: The reproduction of continuous-tone artwork, such as a photograph, by screening the image into dots of various sizes. When printed, the dots merge to give the illusion of continuous tone.

Screen angles: The angles at which halftone screens are placed in order to avoid undesirable screen patterns, called moirés.

Screen ruling: The number of lines or dots per inch in a halftone screen.

Scum: An undesirable film of ink that prints in the nonimage areas of a plate in offset lithography.

Separation: A film negative or positive to be used for each printing plate.

Service bureau: An organization that provides output services to graphic designers and printers in the form of scanning, film output, paper output, and color proofs.

Set back: The predetermined distance from the gripper edge of a press sheet to the beginning of the printed image.

Set-off: The accidental transfer of inked images from one side of a press sheet to the backside of the sheet above or below it.

Shadow: The darkest tones in an image, represented by the largest dots in a halftone.

Sheetfed: A type of printing press that accepts paper in the form of sheets, as opposed to a web-fed press, which accepts paper in the form of webs, or rolls.

Sheetwise: To print one side of the paper with one set of plates, then to turn the sheet over and print the other side with another set of plates.

Show-through: An undesirable condition in printing in which the ink on one side of the paper is visible from the other side under normal lighting conditions.

Side guide: A guide on sheetfed presses that positions the sheet sideways as it feeds into the printing press.

Signature: A group of pages folded together into proper order and alignment.

Skid: A platform that holds a pile of cut sheets.

Soft dot: A dot in photographic images, proofs, and press sheets that has excessive halation around its edges.

Soft proof: A proof of an image or page layout on a computer monitor.

Specification: The characteristics of typeset copy, a color expressed in percentages, or any set of specific instructions for reproducing an image or a page layout.

Spine: The back of a bound book (hard- or softcover) that connects the two covers.

Spot color: A single solid (or screened) color printed using one separation plate, as opposed to a process color printed using two or more separation plates.

Spot varnish: a clear coating applied to a particular area of a printed piece that provides protection as well as a matte or glossy appearance, depending on the type of varnish.

Spread: Two facing pages of a publication.

Step-and-repeat: The process of repeating an image or a group of images by "stepping" it into position using a predetermined measurement.

Stochastic screening: An alternative to conventional screening methods in which an image is color-separated using fine, randomly placed dots rather than geometrically aligned halftone dots.

Stock: The type of paper or other material that will be used for printing.

Stream feeder: The most common type of sheetfed press paper feeders that sends overlapping sheets of paper toward the grippers on a printing press.

Strip: To assemble film on a flat before proofing and platemaking.

Strip in: To manually affix a film negative to another piece of film.

Substrate: The media on which images are proofed or printed.

Subtractive color: Color produced by using cyan, magenta, and yellow inks printed on white paper to absorb, or subtract, the red, green, and blue portions of the spectrum.

Subtractive primaries: Cyan, magenta, yellow, and black (CMYK). The colors used for process color printing inks.

T

Tack: The property of cohesion of particles in printing inks.

Template: A preformatted document that is protected from overwriting and can be used repeatedly to create new documents.

Text paper: Any fine-quality printing paper.

TIFF: Tagged Image File Format. A popular graphics format used to store high-resolution bit-mapped images.

Tile: To break a page or image into smaller units so that it can be printed.

Tint: A solid color that has been screened to less than 100 percent to create a lighter shade.

Tonal range: The difference between the brightest and the darkest tone in a photograph, proof, or printed piece.

Tooth: A characteristic of paper in which the finish is slightly rough, allowing it to readily take printing ink.

Transparent ink: A printing ink that does not conceal the color underneath.

Trapping: A method of overlapping adjoining colors or inks that minimizes the possibility of gaps between two colors.

Trim: To cut the excess paper from the edges of a printed piece after it has been printed, folded, or bound.

Trim mark: Vertical or horizontal lines placed outside the image areas of a press sheet to indicate where the paper should be cut.

Trim size: The size of a printed piece after it has been trimmed.

Two-up: The imposition of two items to be printed on the same press sheet.

U

Uncoated: Paper with no finish coating applied to it.

Underrun: The production of fewer printed pieces than originally specified.

Unders/overs: The amount of printed material that is under or over the originally specified print run.

Unit cost: The price to print per piece.

UV coating: A protective, ultraviolet, transparent finish applied to a printed piece.

V

Vacuum frame: A vacuum device used in proofing and platemaking that holds materials in close contact during exposure.

Varnish: A thin, clear coating applied to a printed piece for protection or special effects.

Vehicle: The fluid component of a printing ink that carries the pigment.

Vellum finish: A toothy paper finish that absorbs ink quickly.

Vendor: A supplier of goods or services, such as a printer, bindery, or a service bureau.

Viscosity: The properties of tack and flow in printing inks.

W

Washup: The process of cleaning the rollers, plates, blankets, and other elements of a printing press after a press run.

Waterless printing: A method of printing without water in which the plates consist of metal for image areas and rubber for non-image areas.

Watermark: A design that is impressed on a sheet of paper during the papermaking process.

Web: A roll of paper used in web printing.

Web press: A printing press that uses rolls (webs) of paper rather than sheets. Also called web-fed press.

Web tension: The amount of pull applied to a web of paper on a web-fed press.

Weight: The density of paper measured in pounds.

Wet trapping: The process of applying layers of ink in rapid succession while the ink is still fluid.

With the grain: To fold or feed paper into a printing press or folding machine parallel to the paper's grain direction.

Work and tumble: The process of printing one side of a sheet of paper, then turning the sheet over from gripper edge to the tail edge, using the same set of plates to print the second side.

Work and turn: The process of printing one side of a sheet of paper, then turning the sheet over from left to right using the same gripper and set of plates to print the second side.

Wove paper: Paper that has a uniform surface and a soft, smooth finish.

Y

Yellow: One of the subtractive primaries (cyan, magenta, yellow, and black) used in four-color process inks.

INDEX

228
...

GRAPHIC
DESIGNER'S
COLOR
HANDBOOK

ART AND PHOTOGRAPHY CREDITS

The following companies supplied artwork used in this book:

ArtToday.com
5232 E. Pima Road
Suite 200C
Tucson, AZ 85712
520/881-8101
http://www.arttoday.com

CMB Design
608 Sutter Street
Suite 200
Folsom, CA 95630
916/605-6500
http://www.cmbdesign.com

Gardner Design
3204 East Douglas
Wichita, KS 67208
316/691-8808
http://www.gardnerdesign.net

Graphic Arts Technical Foundation (GATF)
200 Deer Run Road
Sewickley, PA 15143-2600
412/741-6860 or 800/910-GATF
http://www.gain.net

Heidelberg USA, Inc.
1000 Gutenberg Drive
Kennesaw, GA 30144
888/472-9655
http://www.heidelbergusa.com

Image Wise Packaging
920 24th Street
Sacramento, CA 95816
916/492-9900
John@imagewisepackaging.com

Paul Baker Printing, Inc.
220 Riverside Avenue
Roseville, CA 95678
916/969-8317
http://www.pbaker.com

ACKNOWLEDGMENTS

It's a colorful life no matter where you are, and there are plenty of colorful folks we are indebted to for their humor and support both on a personal and professional level.

For starters, we'd like to send our thanks to Rockport's Kristin Ellison for her patience, professionalism, and hard work. Thank you as well to Stephen Beale, for fine copy editing and technical know-how. A very heartfelt thanks as always to the Blonde Bombshell, whose color is and always shall be, pure gold.

Graphic designers have numerous resources on the Web, but one of the best resources around is ArtToday.com. Many of the images in this book came from ArtToday and over the years, they've been a godsend for many of the projects we've worked on. We'd like to thank them and all of the wonderful artists and photographers whose contributions make this an invaluable site for all designers.

Special thanks to Heidelberg USA for graciously sharing images and cutting edge information, and to the Graphic Arts Technical Foundation (GATF) for granting permission to reproduce elements of their excellent process control forms for commercial printers.

We'd also like to thank Audrey Baker of Paul Baker Printing for sharing practical printing expertise and images.

As with all things in life we'd like to thank our families, Dale, Dottie, Ma, Pop, Pookie, Anne, Terry-Bob, and Kathy.

ABOUT THE AUTHORS

RICK SUTHERLAND

Rick Sutherland is Vice President of Project Development for Lone Wolf Enterprises. In addition to being an author, he has edited dozens of professional texts, including architectural, interior design, landscape design, and engineering books.

Prior to joining Lone Wolf Enterprises, Sutherland was, for 15 years, part-owner of Paul Baker Printing, a multi-million dollar commercial printing company in California, where he served as production foreman, production manager, and for several years as the lead sales account representative.

Sutherland has an extensive printing production background, gleaning years of craftsmanship from master printer, Jake Jacobbsen, and turning that into 10 years of experience as the lead multi-color sheetfed press operator with printing companies focused on advertising agency expectations and quality.

This was preceded by formative years in four-color camera work, film preparation, proofing, and layout. At this time, Sutherland also fell in love with visual media, and began examining where it would lead, and how he would play a part.

He has witnessed the advent of computer-oriented print communications, having received on his desk, only 17 years ago, a stack of 15 floppy disks containing files for a four page brochure from an ad agency courageous enough to submit the first true electronic color files. He remains amazed, proud, and delighted to be part of the process.

BARB KARG

Barb Karg is a 20-year journalist, graphic designer, and screenwriter. Part of desktop publishing since its inception, she has developed many publications from the ground up, and set up complete production and editorial systems for publishers in print and on the Web. As Executive Vice President and Director of Operations of Lone Wolf Enterprises, a professional book production company, she is responsible for overseeing the production and editorial departments. A self-professed publishing "lifer," she holds a B.A. in English and Creative Writing from the University of California, Davis.

Karg's diverse background includes book, magazine, and newspaper production and editorial work. She has served as editor-in-chief for several San Francisco Bay Area publishing companies producing 25 to 65 publications annually, often writing and composing entire publications from start to finish.

Over the years, she has supervised in-house and freelance writers, editors, authors, designers, illustrators, compositors, and photographers. In addition, she has extensive experience in print purchasing, budget preparation, scheduling, working with pre-press operations, and managing computer information systems.

Karg is the author and designer of *Dancing Hamsters, Gothic Garden, and Cyber Conspiracies: The 501 Funniest, Craziest, and Most Bizarre Web Sites You'll Ever See* (Adams Media, Massachusetts, 2000), and co-author and designer of *The Dark Eye: The Official Strategy Guide* (Prima, California, 1986).

Both Karg and Sutherland are based in the Pacific Northwest.